in

RELATIONSHIP

HOW TO ELIMINATE NEGATIVE THINKING,
JEALOUSY, ATTACHMENT AND OVERCOME
COUPLE CONFLICTS. INSECURITY AND FEAR
OF ABANDONMENT OFTEN CAUSE
IRREPARABLE DAMAGE WITHOUT A THERAPY

By **THERESA MILLER**

Congratulation on downloading this ebook, <u>currently best-selling in Anxieties & Phobias category</u>, and thank You for doing so.

Please enjoy !

PRINTED IN USA

ANXIETY SERIES

<u>Anxiety in Relationship</u> has been the first book in the "Anxiety Series", best seller in its category, still today…

The second publication was <u>The Attachment Theory Workbook</u> - How to Eliminate Insecurity in Love, Jealousy, Conflicts and Better Understand your Partenr's Mind. Build a Strong Relationship!

My last effort is <u>Anxious in Love</u> - How Stopping the Spiral of Toxic Thoughts and Anxiety in Relationship Overcoming Conflicts and Insecure of Couple. Abandonment and Separation is Never a Relief! …after many months of absence from publications.

For better enjoyment, you can find all the titles in audio format, <u>on Audible</u>, please!

MY FREE STEP-BY-STEP HELP

<u>I'll send you a free eBook</u>! Yes, you got it right, I'll send you my future projects, in preview, with nothing in return, if you just want a realistic review on them, which I'm sure will be useful to me. Thanks in advance!

Leave me your best email, my staff will send you a copy as soon as possible:

theresamillerauthor@gmail.com

TABLE OF CONTENTS

INTRODUCTION

Relationships between newlyweds at a certain stage could be difficult sometimes, especially when people are struggling with matters of the heart. Most people have had an experience of having to cope with the anxiety arising from suspecting your boyfriend, girlfriend or fiancee of being unfaithful. Of course, most of the time it's not the reality but if these thoughts are not controlled, they might result in over possessiveness of partners, anxiety, obsessions, etc.

Being in a relationship may seem like a bed of roses until, for whatever reason, one gets that gut feeling he/she can't shake, that something just isn't right. You notice that your spouse is behaving a little bit suspicious and this is the most challenging part of a relationship because you get this feeling of doubt which triggers anxiety.

Relationships are usually a lot more intricate than we think they are or desire them to be. Relationships, particularly romantic relations, draw out our unmet needs, anxieties, and unresolved conflicts with people from our past: parents, caretakers, friends, and former relationships.

The relationship with our partners is impacted by our own personal issues. In which case, we often react to our lovers "as if" they were some other person, and quite often, this triggers conflict in the relationship. In highly-charged relationships, we expect love, nurturance, and validation for being who we are. A primary relationship, we normally presume, should provide a healthy environment where we are embraced by our spouses for expressing our own distinctive qualities. Why is this easy expectation so difficult to attain?

The cause could be that how we perceive our spouses are colored by how we learned to communicate with other people over the years. This learning process often starts in early childhood, as early as infancy. The fact is, our initial attachment to a caretaker, a mother, a father, or another adult can affect how we deal with people for our entire lifetime.

If perhaps our initial experiences, for instance, trained us to have a healthy trust in the world, we are very likely tohave a trusting mindset towards people all through our lifetimes. On the other hand, however, if a kid was not shown love and trust during the early stages of life, it might be an issue as an adult to learn how to experience love; this might involve loving one's self.

Touring the route of personal growth, we are exposed to both bad and good memories. Love and trust feel comfortable to us, they both create an optimistic self-image and are positive ways of explaining ourselves as we develop into adulthood. The negative experiences cause feelings of conflicts and dissatisfactions. These bad experiences become an element of self-definition that the person is developing. Nevertheless, these bad thoughts are incompatible with more good feelings. Thus, in accordance with psychodynamic theory, the individual projects these bad feelings onto another individual. For example, criticize your spouse of being controlling when in reality you are the one who bears the need to feel in control.

Projections

As outlined by psychoanalysis, a projection is an unmindful mechanism where one's own mistakes are seen in other persons' rather than in one's own character. In other systems of psychology, a projection is an act of objectifying what is really a subjective or internal experience. The most important thing to bear in mind is that we project our own bad feelings onto someone else. This is especially true in an intimate relationship. If, for example, one partner has that individual will to project the thoughts of jealousy onto the other partner. In other words, if we feel unable to fix the problem in ourselves, we therefore concentrate on the problem in the other person. The way out of this is to discover the process of projection and figure out how it influences you personally.

Often when couples are going through conflict in their relationship, projections tend to be the reason behind the problem. For instance, if we are coping with our own conflicts and are struggling to make any progress in understanding them, we may be psychologically-motivated to look for the problem in the other individual. In fact, on an unconscious level, we might actually look for partners that possess the qualities that we find problematic within ourselves. If we are incapable or reluctant to assert ourselves, we will get furious and frustrated with other people for taking advantage of us. However, we may have chosen spouses who do just that: individuals who control and abuse us. However, our partners may not see themselves as domineering nor abusive, but because you need to work out your own problems with these issues, we will look for these qualities in the other person.

In other words, psychologically, the couples are bound to one another by a mutual agreement, a largely unconscious acceptance of each other. Sharing the same images and unconscious fantasies establish as much an emotional foundation for mutual attraction and passionate attachment as it does for conflict within the couple's relationship. Hence, the mutual unconscious agreement lying at the core of the relationship can become an infrastructure for mutual resilience. These well-known unconscious biases are easily noticeable through all arguments and quarrels. The latent conjunction or agreement between partners usually becomes obvious only after a lengthy therapeutic process.

In the absence of therapeutic interventions, the much healthier alternative is when projections are triggering relationship conflicts to increase your consciousness of your own inner conflicts and how you project these conflicts onto your spouse. When we have awareness of the issue, we can figure out the many ways it impacts our behavior: awareness grants us some control over the problem. As a result, we can then try out different ways to cope with people.

It is important to be aware that projections are not at the root of each problem that couples encounter. In the real world, sometimes the other person does indeed have a real problem that could lead to an abusive situation. In cases like this, it is not wise to try and understand it as a projection, but to see it for what it truly is and to take proper actions to change the situation.

Anxiety and stress can happen in our relationships with others, whether it be our spouse, children, parents, in-laws, co-workers or a host of some other types of relationships. A good and healthy relationship ought to be well-balanced and amicable between both people. When a relationship becomes one-sided, smothering, challenging or disrespectful, it can create a very stressful and anxiety-producing situation.

Any relationship in which the other person does not respect another person's feelings, property or privileges, a person feels violated. The feelings that come from unhealthy relationships result in many emotions such as anger, hostility, depression, resentment as well as an enormous amount of anxiety. In unhealthy couple relationships, anxiety can be quite profound as a partner might feel that they have nowhere to turn and that they must remain committed to the relationship on account of many factors. In abusive relationships, the anxiety and stress are much more obvious as a person is controlled, manipulated and isolated. Someone in these types of unhealthy relationships experiences tremendous amounts of anxiety, wherein they are uncertain of the best way to break free of such a nasty situation. It is equally more stressful when children are involved. A person may also experience anxiety and stress due to other significant others in their family such as relationships with their children, where there are behavioral or discipline issues or a myriad of other factors. There can be issues with extended family, whether it be a controlling in-law or dislike between members of a family. Relationship problems in the workplace with regards to co-workers or bosses can be quite anxiety producing as a person can have a difficult time being productive and motivated in a negative atmosphere in which there is dislike. It is almost impossible to accomplish anything, especially when having to work in such close proximity every day. These are just a few instances to point out but there are many other types of relationships which can be unhealthy and cause a person unnecessary stress.

Unhealthy relationships break down a person's character and create unneeded anxiety and stress that is not felt in healthy relationships. We should seek out healthy relationships as it generates harmony, fulfillment, and happiness. By identifying unhealthy relationships, we can be better prepared in moving towards a more positive direction and eliminating these negative relationships which only stress us out, and create negativity around and within us. Sometimes it is difficult to recognize that you may be in an unhealthy relationship because there are good times to go with the bad, but having the ability to recognize that a relationship is unhealthy is the first step toward happiness and peace.

UNDERSTANDING ANXIETY

Everyone has anxiety. Who hasn't experienced a racing heart, sweaty palms, a jumpy stomach, shortness of breath, trouble sleeping, restlessness or a mind that just won't quiet down? Anxiety is a normal occurrence that alerts the brain and body that something isn't right. It would actually be detrimental if we didn't experience anxiety on occasion because then we might not react appropriately to genuine threats to our safety or well-being.

Even though everyone is subject to occasional anxiety, it can be difficult to watch a loved one struggle with excessive anxiety that clearly interferes with his enjoyment of life. You undoubtedly want the best for your partner, and seeing him be so affected by his worries can be hard. Plus, it can be difficult to protect the relationship and your own quality of life from negative impacts due to your partner's anxieties. This can lead to frustration, anger, sadness, guilt, loneliness, and more. In addition, you may feel sympathy for your partner and overextend yourself in efforts to alleviate his anxiety. You may feel pressured to make everything "just right" but also feel as though you'll never be able to stay one step ahead in preventing or even figuring out what might trigger anxiety for your partner. You may have known all along that your partner had a tendency to be anxious, but living with the effects of that anxiety every day takes a toll.

By reading this book, you're taking steps toward getting a better handle on what's going on with your anxious partner and how you can improve your relationship so that anxiety isn't the focus. No one wants a relationship where every decision is made on the basis of the other person's anxiety. Anxiety puts a lot of limits on life. You and your partner deserve better.

What Is Anxiety?

While we don't know exactly what causes anxiety, we do know that the capacity to feel anxious is biologically hardwired into us. Some people are more susceptible to feeling anxious than others, but there still isn't a definitive biological explanation for this. In addition, how people react to anxiety is a combination of many factors, including genetics, life history, self- esteem, past exposure to stress and trauma, current medical and psychological conditions, and previous experience handling stress, to name just a few. As a result, anxiety is a highly subjective experience, meaning each person feels it uniquely. What may trigger only a mildly anxious feeling in one person can result in a full-blown panic attack in another.

Anxiety is considered an emotion, and like most emotions, it can vary in intensity. At low levels, anxiety is adaptive, meaning that it drives positive outcomes, such as encouraging you to pay your bills on time or to work a few extra hours in order to meet a deadline. Higher anxiety levels, on the other hand, can set off a chain of events that can have significant negative physical and psychological effects. One thing that distinguishes adaptive, "everyday" anxiety from more problematic anxiety and diagnosable anxiety disorders is whether the anxiety resolves when the stressful situation is over or continues even in the absence of an imminent threat. Let's take a closer look at common anxiety symptoms and what those signs mean.

Common Anxiety Symptoms

Although the experience of anxiety is highly individualized, certain physical, behavioral, and emotional symptoms are common, as are certain thought patterns. As you read the following sections, think about whether you've observed any of these signs in your partner when he's feeling anxious.

Physical Signs of Anxiety

Common physical symptoms of anxiety include a racing heart, excessive perspiration, trembling or shaking, feeling restless, fatigue or problems sleeping, shortness of breath, chest pain or tightness, nausea or diarrhea, upset stomach or butterflies in the stomach, dizziness, chills or hot flushes, and numbness. Another physical sign is an exaggerated response when startled, like jumping a mile if someone says something to you from behind when you didn't know anyone was there. It's important to note that these symptoms are natural responses to normal anxiety and don't necessarily mean someone has an anxiety disorder. However, the severity, duration, and effects of these symptoms are key factors in determining whether people are experiencing an anxiety disorder or just a typical response to anxiety.

Behavioral Signs of Anxiety

How your partner acts when he's experiencing anxiety can offer a lot of clues about what's going on with him internally. Some common behaviors of people who are anxious include:

- Avoiding places or events that trigger anxiety, such as bridges, elevators, or parties; fleeing situations that make them uncomfortable, such as a movie theater or crowded restaurant.

- Performing compulsive behaviors repeatedly, such as washing their hands time and time again or checking the door locks a precise number of times before going to bed.

- Limiting outside activities by not leaving home or only going to a few specific "safe" places.

- Engaging in risky, self-destructive behaviors, such as drinking or taking drugs.

Ironically, even though your partner may feel as if these behaviors reduce his anxiety, they actually make it worse.

Emotional Signs of Anxiety

As previously mentioned, anxiety is an emotion, and it can evoke a lot of different feelings. Common words your partner might use when trying to describe his experience of anxiety are "worry," "apprehension," "fear," "dread," "uneasiness," "distress," "feeling overwhelmed," "panic," "pressure," "terror," "jumpiness," "stress," and "edginess." Your partner may also say he can't describe what he's feeling or might simply say, "Something isn't right." These emotional responses to anxiety often arise due to thought patterns common among people with anxiety, so let's take a look at those.

Common Thoughts That Signal Anxiety

The thoughts people experience when feeling anxious are commonly referred to as "worry." Everyone worries sometimes, but people who are experiencing persistent anxiety have more worry thoughts than typical and struggle to think of other things. Here are some common worry thoughts:

- What if____happens?

- I can't cope with this.

- I'll never be able to handle____.

- This is too much for me. I'm going to fail.

- I have to be in control.

- I might as well give up now. This isn't going to work, no matter how hard I try.

- Everyone is going to laugh at me.

- I must be going crazy!

Again, people can have these thoughts and not have an anxiety disorder. To understand the distinction, let's take a look at the difference between "everyday" anxiety and a diagnosable anxiety disorder.

"Everyday" Anxiety vs. Anxiety Disorders

It can be a fine line to distinguish between "everyday" anxiety and a diagnosable condition. Often, the distinction hinges on whether people describe symptoms of anxiety that interfere with their quality of life and if these symptoms are pervasive, and negatively impact their performance (whether that's in one area of life or across all situations).

For example, if your partner has a big presentation coming up at work soon and has been working extremely hard to pull it together, he might be feeling anxious. Symptoms of that anxiety might include having trouble sleeping, being irritable and impatient, and having worry thoughts about what might go wrong. This could be "everyday" anxiety, or it could be a sign of an anxiety disorder, depending on how long the symptoms have been going on, the severity of the symptoms, and whether they resolve after he gives the presentation. If his symptoms do go away afterward, he was probably experiencing "everyday" anxiety in response to a stressful situation. If he still struggles with his symptoms afterward and also feels anxious about other life situations, it might be a sign of an anxiety disorder.

Anxiety And Relationships: Proven Ways To Eliminate It

Intimate relationships are a mirror, reflecting the best and the worst of all of us. They can inflame our struggles or soothe them. When they're right, they can feel like magic but even when they're completely right, anxiety can steal the magic and loosen the connection between two people who belong together. All relationships require trust, tenderness, patience, and vulnerability. People with anxiety often have these by the truckload and will give them generously to the relationship. The problem is that anxiety can sometimes just as quickly erode them.

If you're someone who struggles with anxiety, there are plenty of things about you that would make loving you easy. All relationships struggle sometimes and when anxiety is at play, the struggles can be quite specific – very normal, and specific.

Anxiety can work in curious ways, and it will impact different relationships differently, so not all of the following will be relevant for every relationship. Here are some ways to strengthen your relationship and protect it from the impact of anxiety:

1.   Top Up The Emotional Resources

You're probably super sensitive to the needs of others and give openly and abundantly to your relationship. Sometimes though, anxiety can drain those resources from the relationship just as quickly as you invest them. This is completely okay – there is plenty of good that comes with loving you to make up for this – but it may mean that you have to keep making sure those resources are topped up. Whenever you can, heap your partner with attention, gratitude, affection, touch – lots of touch – and conversation around him or her.

2. Let Your Partner See You As a Support Too

Your partner might feel reluctant to 'burden' you with worries, particularly if those worries don't seem as big as the ones you're struggling with. People with anxiety have so much strength – it's impossible to live with anxiety without it – so make sure your partner knows that it doesn't matter how big or small their struggles are, you can be the supportive one sometimes too. The tendency can be for partners of anxious people to dismiss their own worries, but this might mean that they do themselves out of the opportunity to feel nurtured and supported by you – which would be a huge loss for both of you. Be deliberate in being the rock sometimes too. Ask, hold, touch. There's nothing more healing than the warmth of the person you love.

3. Let Your Partner In On What You're Thinking

Anxious thoughts are supremely personal, but let your partner in on them. It's an important part of intimacy. You will often be thinking about what you need to do to feel safe, what feels bad for you and what could go wrong. You will also have an enormous capacity to think of other people – anxious people do – but make sure that you let your partner in on the thoughts that arrest you. Keeping things too much to yourself has a way of widening the distance between two people.

4. Asking For Reassurance Is Absolutely Okay – But Just Not Too Much

Anxiety has a way of creeping into everything.

When it's left unchecked, it can make you doubt the things that don't deserve to be doubted – such as your relationship. It's completely okay and very normal to ask your partner for reassurance. However, if it is done too much, it could be felt as neediness. Neediness is the enemy of desire and over time can smother the spark. Make sure your partner has the opportunity to love you spontaneously, without prompting – it's lovely for them and even better for you.

5.   Be Vulnerable

Anxiety can affect relationships in different ways. In some people, it might stoke the need for constant reassurance. In others, it can cause them to hold back so as to lessen their vulnerability to possible heartache. Vulnerability – being open to another – is beautiful and it's the essence of successful, healthy relationships. The problem with protecting yourself too much is that it can invite the very rejection you're trying to protect against. Part of intimacy is letting someone in closer than you let the rest of the world. It's trusting that person with the fragile, messy, untamed parts of you – the parts that are often beautiful, sometimes baffling, and always okay with the person who loves you. It's understandable to worry about what might happen if someone has open access to these parts of you, but see those worries for what they are – worries, not realities – and trust that whatever happens when you open yourself up to loving and being loved, you'll be okay. Because you will be.

6.   Be Careful Of Projecting Anxiety Onto Your Relationship

Anxiety can be triggered by nothing in particular – that's one of the awful things about it – so it will look for a target, an anchor to hold it still and make it make sense. If you're in an intimate relationship, that's where the bullseye will sit, drawing your anxiety into its gravitational pull. This can raise feelings of doubt, jealousy, suspicion, and insecurity. Anxiety can be a rogue like that. That doesn't mean your relationship deserves your anxiety – most likely it doesn't – but your relationship is important, relevant and often in your thoughts, making it an extremely easy target. Remind yourself that just because you're worried, that doesn't mean there's anything to worry about. Worry if you have to, but then see it for what it is – anxiety, not truth. You are loved and you have anxiety and you are okay. Let that be the truth that holds you.

7.   Analysis Leads To Paralysis

There's a saying – 'Analysis leads to paralysis,' – because it does. 'Is it love? Or lust? Or am I kidding myself? What if my heart gets broken into tiny jagged pieces? How will it ever work if we don't like the same music, books, food or movies? What if we book the holiday and the airline goes on strike? What if one of us gets sick? What if both of us get sick? What if we can't get a refund? Or pay the mortgage? What if he gets sick of me?' Yep. I know you know how it sounds. What you focus on is what becomes important, so if you focus on the possible problems, they'll absorb your energy until they're big enough to cause trouble on their own.

They'll drain your energy, your sense of fun and your capacity to move. You probably already know this, but what to do about it. Here's something to try... Set a time frame in which you can act as though things will be fine. So for example, worry from 10-3 each day and after that, breathe, let go and act as though things will be fine. You don't have to believe it – just 'act as if you do.' You'll have another chance tomorrow to worry if you need to. Be guided by the evidence, not the worries that haunt you at 2 am.

8.   Come Closer. No. Go Away

When you focus on every detail, things will get wobbly. You might focus on the things that aren't right with your partner or your relationship, while at the same time looking for reassurance that your partner loves you and is committed. This can cause you to push your partner away, ("You've disappointed me,") then pull him or her close, ("Tell me that you love me. You do love me, don't you?"). Have a chat with your partner and if it is a familiar process, set up a safe way for your partner to point out when it's happening. Agree on what that will look like. When it does happen, be careful not to hear it as a criticism – it's not – it's your partner asking for some stability with the way you love each other.

9. The Tough Conversations Can Bring You Closer

All relationships have to deal with tough stuff now and then but anxiety can make things more threatening and bigger than they are. The temptation might be to avoid talking about difficult issues with your partner, because of concerns about what it might do the relationship. Difficult issues don't go away – they fester until they reach boiling point. Trust that your partner – and you – can cope with a hard discussion. Relationships are built on trust, and trusting that your relationship can power through difficult conversations is an important one.

10. Let Your Partner In On What It's Like To Be You

We, humans, are complex creatures and bringing someone in closer to you and your story – even if it is someone who has been with you for a while – is the lifeblood of intimacy. People change, stories change, and even in intimate relationships, it's easy to lose touch with the person who falls asleep next to you at nights. Let your partner in on what your anxiety is like for you. Talk about your thoughts, how anxiety is affecting you, your work, your relationship, your partner, and how grateful you are for the love and support.

11. Let Your Partner Know What Triggers You

Is there a particular situation that tends to set your anxiety alight? Crowds? Strangers? Difficulties of exit? Loud music in the car? Being late? Talk to your partner so that if you find yourself in the situation without warning, he or she will understand what's happening with you.

12. Be Patient. The Quick Fix Isn't Always The Best

As a way to feel better and ease your anxiety, you might be tempted to press for a quick fix to a problem or issue within your relationship. You might become frustrated with your partner's desire to wait or put off committing to a course of action, or their resistance to keep talking about the issue, but be open to the fact that your partner might see things differently, sometimes clearer. Breathe, talk, and don't assume that your partner is taking time or pulling out of the conversation because of a lack of commitment or because the issue isn't important enough.

13. Make Sure You're Looking After Yourself

Being in love is crazy good but it can take your attention away from looking after yourself and on to looking after your special person. We all tend to do this but for people with anxiety, it can be particularly problematic because once you're off-balance, the ripple can make other things undone. Taking good care of yourself is so important. Eating well (a healthy diet rich in omega 3, low in processed carbs and sugars), as well as regular exercise and meditation will help to build your brain against anxiety. If looking after yourself feels selfish, think of it this way: it's not really fair to expect your partner to support you through your anxiety if you're not doing everything you can do to support yourself. Think of self-care as an investment in you, your relationship and your partner. Remember too that anything that's good for anxiety is good for everyone, so talk to your partner about chasing a healthy lifestyle together – cooking, exercising and meditating together.

14. Understand That Your Partner Will Need Boundaries

For the relationship to stay close, healthy and connected, boundaries built by your partner can be a great thing. Understand that boundaries aren't your partner's way of keeping you out but as a way to self-protect from 'catching' your anxiety. You might be worried and need to talk about something over and over, but that's not necessarily what will be good for you, your partner or your relationship. Your partner can love you and draw a bold heavy underline between the last time you discuss something and the next time you want to. Talking is healthy, but talking over and over about the same thing can be draining and create an issue where there isn't one. Know that your partner loves you and that boundaries are important to nurture love and grow the relationship, not to push against it. Talk to your partner about what he or she needs to be able to feel okay in the face of your anxiety. Invite the boundaries – it will help to keep your connection strong and loving and will help your partner to feel as though he or she is able to preserve a sense of self without being absorbed by your worries. Worrying is contagious, so if your partner wants to draw a boundary (eventually) around your worry, let it happen – it will help to preserve the emotional resources of the relationship and will be good for both of you.

15.   Laugh Together

This is so important! Laughter is a natural antidote to the stress and tension that comes with anxiety. Laughing together will tighten the connection between you and when there have been a stressful few days, weeks or months, it will help you both to remember why you fell in love with each other. Anxiety has a way of making you forget that life wasn't meant to be taken seriously all the time. If it's been too long since your partner has seen the shape of your face when you laugh (which will be beautiful and probably one of the reasons he or she fell for you in the first place) find a reason – a funny movie, memories, YouTube... anything.

Falling in love is meant to be magical, but getting close to another person isn't without its highs and lows at the best of times. From the ecstasy of realizing that someone pretty wonderful is as moved by you as you are by them, to the agony of self-doubt and possible loss, to the security, richness and sometimes stillness of a deeper love, intimacy is a vehicle for every possible emotion. Anxiety does affect relationships, but by being open to its impact, and deliberate in responding to it, you can protect your relationship and make it one that's strong, close and resilient.

GETTING OVER RELATIONSHIP
INSECURITY

"She isn't attracted to me anymore. She never acts as excited to see me when I come home. Why can't it just be like it was in the beginning?" My friend has just entered into the first of two common phases of relationship insecurity: rhetorical questioning. The internal investigation continues with, "She takes forever to answer my texts. Doesn't she miss me when I'm gone? She used to always laugh at my jokes. Do you think she's interested in someone else?"

Then comes phase two: turning on himself - "It's because I'm losing my looks. I'm away too often. She doesn't think I'm fun anymore. I can't make her happy. There's something wrong with me. She wants someone better."

We've all most likely been at one or the other ends of this scenario; we've either been the worrier or been with the worrier. Chances are, we've actually experienced both. Insecurity, as most of us know firsthand, can be toxic to our closest relationships. And while it can bounce back and forth from partner to partner, both the cause of our insecurity and its cure reside in us alone.

Unsurprisingly, studies have found that people with low self-esteem have more relationship insecurities, which can prevent them from experiencing the benefits of a loving relationship. People with low self-esteem not only want their partner to see them in a better light than they see themselves but in moments of self-doubt, they have trouble even recognizing their partner's affirmations. Moreover, the very acting out of our insecurities can push our partner away, thus creating a self-fulfilling prophecy. Because this struggle is so internal and most of the time even independent of circumstances, it's important to deal with our insecurities without distorting or dragging our partner into them. We can do this by taking three steps:

- Uncovering the real roots of our insecurity

- Examining the signs of insecurity in our relationships

- Challenging the inner critic that sabotages our relationship.

1. Where does our insecurity come from?

Nothing awakens distant hurts like a close relationship. Our relationships stir up old feelings from our past more than anything else. Our brains are even flooded with the same neurochemical in both situations.

We all have working models for relationships that were formed in our early attachments to influential caretakers. Whatever our early pattern was, it shapes our adult relationships. Our style of attachment influences which partners we choose and the dynamics that play out in our relationships. A secure attachment pattern helps a person to be more confident and self-possessed. However, when someone has an anxious or preoccupied attachment style, they may be more likely to feel insecure toward their partner.

Knowing our attachment style is beneficial because it can help us to realize ways we may be recreating a dynamic from our past. It can help us to choose better partners and form healthier relationships, which can actually, in turn, change our attachment style. Finally, it can make us more aware of how our feelings of insecurity may be misplaced, based on something old as opposed to our current situation.

Our insecurities can further stem from a "critical inner voice" that we've internalized based on negative programming from our past. If we had a parent who hated themselves, for example, or who directed critical attitudes toward us, we tend to internalize this point of view and carry it with us like a cruel coach inside our heads. This inner critic tends to be very vocal about the things that really matter to us, like our relationships. Take the example of my friend, mentioned above. First, the critical inner voice fueled doubts about his girlfriend's interest in him, then it turned on him. The second he perceived the situation through the filter of his critical inner voice, which told him his girlfriend was pulling away, his mind flooded with terrible thoughts toward himself. One minute, he was just fine. The next minute, he was listening to an inner voice telling him all the ways he couldn't measure up and that he was being rejected.

Relationships shake us up. They challenge the core feelings we have about ourselves and evict us from long-lived-in comfort zones. They tend to turn up the volume of our inner voice and reopen unresolved wounds from our past. If we felt abandoned as a child, the aloof behavior of a romantic partner won't just feel like a current frustration. It also has the potential to send us back into the emotional state of a terrified child, who needed our parent/s for survival. As hard as it may feel to connect our contemporary reactions with beliefs, attitudes, and experiences from our early lives, it is an invaluable tool for getting to know ourselves, and ultimately, for challenging behaviors that don't serve us or even fit with our real, adult life.

2. Three signs of insecurity

We can't always account for every unknown variable in a relationship, so when there's trouble, insecurity appears in relationships. Whether it's on his side or her side, the symptoms are relatively the same. At first, it may be hard to accept and we may even deny the problem in the relationship but that's the last thing you want to do. Below are three signs you should be aware of and act on as soon as possible.

Being Too Defensive - For men, this may be the least present sign of insecurity in a relationship. Being overly sensitive about what she says can be negative in your relationship. If you can't take a joke or criticism, you can be sure the relationship isn't going to last very long. If pride or ego is what's keeping you, throw it away. You'll find your partner is much likely to appreciate you more if you can be a man about these sort of things.

Being Irrationally Jealous - Checking up on her and calling her every five minutes is just about the same as stalking her. She doesn't like it: you're only exhausting yourself and she'll probably get a restraining order at some point. Insecurity in relationships is caused by a lack of trust. If you're being overly protective of her, she'll just assume you don't trust her enough to make the right decisions. Unless she wants to date her father, she probably wants to be able to make her own decisions. So let her. You're not going to always be around her, so if you become jealous every single time she's out by herself, you're setting yourself up for a really bad breakup.

Being Too Materialistic - The worst insecurity in relationships is being too materialistic. If you're so worried about what you wear or own to impress her, then there's a problem. Not only do you lack the confidence in your relationship, but much likely depend on your income to keep your relationship. This is very bad because your income is crucial to your survival. Relationships come and go. Can you afford to do the same with your income? Didn't think so. Buying a nice watch or nice clothes is not a bad thing. However, don't depend on these items to impress her. Instead, impress her with your knowledge as long as it's not money related.

3.   How to Deal With Relationship Insecurity

In order to challenge our insecurity, we have to first get to know our critical inner voice. We should try to catch it each and every time creeps into our minds. Sometimes, it may be easy. We're getting dressed to go out on a date, and it screeches, "You look awful! You're so fat. Just cover yourself up. He'll never be attracted to you." Other times, it'll be more sneaky, even soothing sounding, "Just keep to yourself. Don't invest or show her how you feel, and you won't get hurt." This voice can even turn on our partner in ways that make us feel more insecure, saying, "You can't trust him. He's probably cheating on you!" Identifying this critical inner voice is the first step to challenging it. Here you can learn specific steps you can take to conquer this inner critic and keep it from infiltrating your love life.

As we start to challenge these negative attitudes toward ourselves, we must also make an effort to take actions that go against the directives of our critical inner voice. In terms of a relationship, that means not acting out based on unwarranted insecurities or acting in many ways we don't respect. Here are some helpful steps to take:

Maintain your independence. It's crucial to keep a sense of ourselves separate from our partner. The goal for a relationship should be to make a fruit salad and not a smoothie. In other words, we shouldn't forego essential parts of who we are in order to become merged into a couple. Instead, each of us should work to maintain the unique aspects of ourselves that attracted us to each other in the first place, even as we move closer. In this way, each of us can hold strong, knowing that we are a whole person in and of ourselves.

Don't act out, no matter how anxious you are. Of course, this is easier said than done, but we all know our insecurities can precipitate some pretty destructive behavior. Acts of jealousy or possessiveness can hurt our partners, not to mention us. Snooping through their text messages, calling every few minutes to see where they are, getting mad every time they look at another attractive person - these are all acts that we can avoid, no matter how anxious it makes us, and in the end, we will feel much stronger and more trusting. Even more importantly, we will be trustworthy.

Because we can only change our half of the dynamic, it's always valuable to think about if there are any actions we take that push our partner away. If we're acting in a way we respect, and we still don't feel like we're getting what we want, we can make a conscious decision to talk about it with our partner or change the situation, but we never have to feel victimized or allow ourselves to act in ways that we don't respect.

Don't seek reassurance. Expecting our partner to reassure us when we feel insecure only leads to more insecurities. Remember, these attitudes come from inside us, and unless we can overcome them within ourselves, it won't matter how smart, sexy, worthy or attractive our partner tells us we are. No matter what, we must strive to feel okay within ourselves. This means really and fully accepting the love and affection our partner directs toward us. Looking to our partner at every turn for reassurance to prove we are okay adds a burden that weighs on them and detracts from ourselves.

Stop measuring. It's important not to constantly evaluate or assess our partner's every move. We have to accept that our partner is a separate person with a sovereign mind. We won't always see things the same way or express our love in the same way. This doesn't mean we should settle for someone who doesn't offer us what we want in a relationship, but when we do find someone who we value and love, we should try not to enter into a tit-for-tat mentality in which we continuously measure who owes who what and when.

A relationship should be equal in terms of maturity and kindnesses exchanged. If things feel off, we can communicate clearly what we want, but we shouldn't expect our partner to read our minds or know exactly what to do all the time. As soon as we get into the blame game, it's a hard cycle from which to break free.

Go all in. We all have anxiety, but we can increase our tolerance for the many ambiguities that every relationship inevitably presents by being true to ourselves. We can invest in a person even when we know they have the power to hurt us. Keeping one foot out the door only keeps the relationship from becoming as close as it can and may even undermine it altogether. When we allow ourselves to be loved and to feel loving, we are bound to also feel anxious, but sticking it out has more rewards than we may imagine. When we take a chance without letting our insecurities dictate our behavior, the best case scenario is that the relationship blossoms and the worst case is that we grow within ourselves. No time is wasted that taught us something about ourselves or that helped nourish our capacity to love and be vulnerable.

HOW YOUR ATTACHMENT STYLE
IMPACTS YOUR RELATIONSHIP

Our style of attachment affects everything from our partner selection to how well our relationships progress and to, sadly, how they end. That is why recognizing our attachment pattern can help us understand our strengths and vulnerabilities in a relationship. An attachment pattern is established in early childhood and continues to function as a working model for relationships in adulthood. This model of attachment influences how each of us reacts to our needs and how we go about getting them met. When there is a secure attachment pattern, a person is confident and self-possessed and is able to easily interact with others, meeting both their own and another's needs. However, when there is an anxious or avoidant attachment pattern and a person picks a partner who fits with that maladaptive pattern, they will most likely be choosing someone who isn't the ideal choice to make them happy.

For example, the person with a working model of anxious/preoccupied attachment feels that in order to get close to someone and have your needs met, you need to be with your partner all the time and get reassurance. To support this perception of reality, they choose someone who is isolated and hard to connect with. The person with a working model of dismissive/avoidant attachment has the tendency to be distant because their model is that the way to get your needs met is to act like you don't have any. He or she then chooses someone who is more possessive or overly demanding of attention. In a sense, we set ourselves up by finding partners that confirm our models. If we grew up with an insecure attachment pattern, we may project or seek to duplicate similar patterns of relating as adults, even when these patterns hurt us and are not in our own self-interest.

In their research, Dr. Phillip Shaver and Dr. Cindy Hazan found that about 60 percent of people have a secure attachment, while 20 percent have an avoidant attachment, and 20 percent have an anxious attachment.

So what does this mean? There are questions you can ask yourself to help you determine your style of attachment and how it is affecting your relationships. You can start to identify your own attachment style by getting to know the four patterns of attachment in adults and learning how they commonly affect couples in their relating with each other.

Secure Attachment - Securely attached adults tend to be more satisfied in their relationships. Children with a secure attachment see their parent as a secure base from which they can venture out independently to explore the world. A secure adult has a similar relationship with their romantic partner: feeling secure and connected while allowing themselves and their partner to move freely.

Secure adults offer support when their partner feels distressed. They also go to their partner for comfort when they themselves feel troubled. Their relationship tends to be honest, open and eQual, with both people feeling independent, yet loving toward each other. Securely attached couples don't tend to engage in what my father, a psychologist, describes as a "Fantasy Bond," an illusion of connection that provides a false sense of safety. In a fantasy bond, a couple foregoes real acts of love for a more routine, emotionally cut-off form of relating.

Anxious-Preoccupied Attachment - Unlike securely attached couples, people with an anxious attachment tend to be desperate to form a fantasy bond. Instead of feeling real love or trust toward their partner, they often feel emotional hunger. They're frequently looking to their partner to rescue or complete them. Although they're seeking a sense of safety and security by clinging to their partner, they take actions that push their partner away.

Even though anxiously attached individuals act desperate or insecure, more often than not, their behavior exacerbates their own fears. When they feel unsure of their partner's feelings and unsafe in their relationship, they often become clingy, demanding or possessive toward their partner. They may also interpret independent actions by their partner as an affirmation of their fears. For example, if their partner starts socializing more with friends, they may think, "See? He doesn't really love me. This means he is going to leave me. I was right not to trust him."

Dismissive-Avoidant Attachment - People with a dismissive-avoidant attachment have the tendency to emotionally distance themselves from their partner. They may seek isolation and feel "pseudo-independent," taking on the role of parenting themselves. They often come off as focused on themselves and maybe overly attending to their creature comforts. Pseudo-independence is an illusion, as every human being needs connection. Nevertheless, people with a dismissive-avoidant attachment tend to lead more inward lives, both denying the importance of loved ones and detaching easily from them. They are often psychologically defended and have the ability to shut down emotionally. Even in heated or emotional situations, they are able to turn off their feelings and not react. For example, if their partner is distressed and threatens to leave them, they would respond by saying, "I don't care."

Fearful-Avoidant Attachment - A person with a fearful-avoidant attachment lives in an ambivalent state of being afraid of being both too close to or too distant from others. They attempt to keep their feelings at bay but are unable to; they can't just avoid their anxiety or run away from their feelings. Instead, they are overwhelmed by their reactions and often experience emotional storms. They tend to be mixed up or unpredictable in their moods. They see their relationships from the working model that you need to go toward others to get your needs met, but if you get close to others, they will hurt you. In other words, the person they want to go to for safety is the same person they are frightened to be close to. As a result, they have no organized strategy for getting their needs met by others.

As adults, these individuals tend to find themselves in rocky or dramatic relationships, with many highs and lows. They often have fears of being abandoned but also struggle with being intimate. They may cling to their partner when they feel rejected, then feel trapped when they are close. Oftentimes, the timing seems to be off between them and their partner. A person with fearful avoidant attachment may even wind up in an abusive relationship.

The good news is, it's never too late to develop a secure attachment. The attachment style you developed as a child based on your relationship with a parent or early caretaker doesn't have to define your ways of relating to those you love in your adult life. If you come to know your attachment style, you can uncover ways you are defending yourself from getting close and being emotionally connected and work toward forming an "earned secure attachment."

One essential way to do this is by making sense of your story. Attachment research demonstrates that "the best predictor of a child's security of attachment is not what happened to his parents as children, but rather how his parents made sense of those childhood experiences." The key to "making sense" of your life experiences is to write a coherent narrative, which helps you understand how your childhood experiences are still affecting you in your life today.

You can also challenge your defenses by choosing a partner with a secure attachment style, and work on developing yourself in that relationship. Therapy can also be helpful for changing maladaptive attachment patterns. By becoming aware of your attachment style, both you and your partner can challenge the insecurities and fears supported by your age-old working models and develop new styles of attachment for sustaining a satisfying, loving relationship.

JEALOUSY IN MARRIAGE: WHY IT HAPPENS AND DEALING WITH IT

A little jealousy gives a relationship some spice, but too much jealousy can be destructive in any romantic relationship. Jealousy occurs when a spouse feels threatened by a third person whom he or she believes is a rival and a threat to their relationship. Jealousy can either be healthy or unhealthy and it can be either be based on real threats or just imagined threats. Unhealthy jealousy, which is usually unnecessary and unreasonable, can ruin a marriage.

When jealousy becomes unhealthy?

Jealousy is healthy when it pushes couples to be more loving, more sensitive and committed to each other because they value each other too much that they don't want to lose one another. Unhealthy jealousy, on the other hand, makes the relationship troubled. Unhealthy jealousy or unnecessary accusations of infidelity pushes the jealous spouse to think and act irrationally. Extreme jealousy can push a spouse to have irrational thoughts and display unacceptable behaviors. These unacceptable behaviors may include stalking the accused spouse, checking and monitoring the accused spouse's personal belongings like phones, clothes, bags, diaries, social media accounts, etc. for evidences of sexual infidelity, cutting off spouse's relationship with friends, unexpected visits to spouse's workplace, confronting or interrogating the spouse and the worst is committing violence to make the accused spouse confess.

Whether you are the jealous partner or whether your spouse is the jealous one, irrational jealousy can eventually destroy your marriage. Here are answers to frequent questions about jealousy and things you can do to overcome jealousy in your marriage.

Is Jealousy Natural?

In relationships where feelings of jealousy are mild and occasional, it reminds the couple not to take each other for granted. It can encourage couples to appreciate each other and make a conscious effort to make sure the other person feels valued. Jealousy heightens emotions, making love feel stronger and sex more passionate. In small, manageable doses, jealousy can be a positive force in a relationship. But when it's intense or irrational, the story is very different. Occasional jealousy is natural and can keep a relationship alive, but when it becomes intense or irrational, it can seriously damage a relationship.

What Do Jealous People Feel?

Jealous individuals experience a multitude of feelings including fear, anger, humiliation, sense of failure, feeling suspicious, threatened, rage, grief, worry, envy, sadness, doubt, pain, and self-pity.

Jealousy keeps us under a sense of discouraging frustration and disappointment. It makes us gloomy. It is such a depressing feeling that we cannot talk about it with even our best friends nor can we contain it within ourselves. Consequently, it leaves us with an inconvenience of a peculiar misery and if allowed to grow unchecked beyond a limit, it works like a slow poison to our healthy nature.

Dealing With Unhealthy Jealousy

As much as we would like to deny it, most people struggle with jealous emotions at some point in their lives and, in marriage, it is one of those common marriage problems that can develop from feelings of insecurity or neglect. We now live in a society where marriages may not be the first relationship we have had. In some cultures, dating starts in the teenage years and today, subsequent marriages are common. This is just society as we now know it. Many couples may enter into a relationship with their previous baggage and find it hard to settle into a secure, trusting environment. Insecurity is often heightened if a previous partner is still around, where one or both partners are consumed with social media or where the couple live separate lives with one person out all the time working and socializing and the other longing for company and attention at home. Overcoming insecurities and building self-confidence is something that I frequently cover in my online coaching sessions, for others it is purely letting go of jealousy. If you are experiencing jealosy in your relationship or you are the one with jealousy, my heart goes out to you because it's a hard place to be. Jealousy in relationships can develop from numerous situations and no matter how much you try and tell yourself there is no need for concern, your mind just doesn't listen. This worsens at times when your partner continues with the behavior that is instilling the feeling of insecurity throughout your very soul. Below are the common triggers, but for some I coach, there are no triggers.

The four most common triggers of jealousy I see includes flirting, infidelity, long working hours, and the arrival of children, so I have outlined them as well.

Triggers of Jealousy

1.   Long Working Hours

Too much time at work can leave your partner feeling very insecure, especially when your hours at work increase and you spend less and less time at home for the sake of your family. Some may question if it is really for the sake of the family. It is not for me to judge and neither should you judge yourself or your relationship unless it is causing a problem. I see all too often people getting fixated on their goals and have no idea how this impacts their relationship and their family life. This is what happened to me; I became so focused on my previous job's targets and exercise regime that I neglected my relationship and personal life. It's easily done. I still can't believe that I spent over 14 hours a day exercising and working, 6 days a week. If I loved my job then maybe it wouldn't matter so much but I didn't. So it depends on your priorities and passion whether you choose or need to work long hours. But if it is causing problems such as jealousy, you may want to reevaluate and get more balance. For long hours to not be an issue, you both must see its benefits and make time for connection.

2.   Natural Flirts

Some people are natural flirts and notice attractive people when they walk into a room. Natural flirts can often draw the opposite sex like magnets, which can leave the other insecure and just waiting for the moment when they are dumped for the next person that comes along. The partner who flirts often has no idea what impact their actions have on their relationship. They don't actually believe that they are doing anything wrong but perceive their actions to be friendly and not harmful. Yasser was a natural flirt and Arwa couldn't stand it: she played up so many scenarios in her mind and it was affecting her sleep. We had a session where he agreed to tame it down and show more affection to her. I then spent a few sessions with her, helping her not to take his behavior personally and to recognize that flirting doesn't mean he loves her any less. She admitted that she married him that way and hoped he may change after marriage. In my experience working with many people, it is hard to change someone else and part of loving someone is accepting them for who they are.

3.   New Baby Arrival

Jealousy can arise if husbands feel neglected when a new baby arrives, no matter how much they wanted the child in the first place. A baby's mere existence is totally life changing with more attention towards the child and a complete 'nose dive' in marital relations. With the bond between mother and child being that much closer (on average), it can leave fathers feeling neglected, unwanted and a total spare part.

With some of my coaching clients, the jealousy around children actually worked the other way. Katy felt totally trapped after the birth of their first child and her husband David spent all his time looking after the baby. She just yearned for the life they had prior to children when they traveled, enjoyed a good social life and spent all their free time together.

No Trigger for Jealousy

Whilst there are many other causes of jealousy, too many to mention here, there are also those I work with who tell me "I know I have nothing to be jealous for but I cannot help i.t" They say, "My wife is open and honest about everything. We share a joint email address, I have her Facebook password and yet I can't help thinking she is with someone else when I am away and I don't like it when she goes out at night without me."

Another client said to me, "I know my jealousy is down to my insecurities around the way I look. My boyfriend is wonderful and understands it, but I am scared I am driving him away with my obsessive mistrust." When there is clearly no trigger, we must look at where it comes from and take action to our boost self-confidence and most importantly, change our thought patterns.

Tips to Deal with Jealousy

Jealousy in and of itself is not a bad thing: it's a strong indication that you really care. The main thing we need to remember is not to let the jealousy consume, arouse fury and become destructive. If you are suffering from feelings of jealousy then I have outlined some steps below.

1. Start by questioning yourself

Look at the cause, question your feelings and determine whether they have any foundation. Is your partner actually doing anything wrong, have they really done anything to drive your jealous emotions or have you just let your emotions spiral out of control? Then decide if it's you or their behavior that needs to change.

2. If it's you - reassure yourself

If you realize that perhaps it is you overreacting, my heart goes out to you. Most of us have all been there at some time on some level. The fact that you acknowledge this is a great step. Does it come from past experiences? Is it linked to insecurities, fears of being rejected or not having control?

3.   Ask yourself and recognize where this is coming from

Write your thoughts down - getting them out of your head on to paper or tablet can help.

Write a list of all positive examples the behavior could mean, for example - they haven't called because they can't or are busy as opposed to 'they are ignoring me because they are with someone else" or "I know how important and demanding their work is. Their coming home late is not about me, so I vow to not take it personally."

4.   Write a list of all the reasons trust is important to you and to a relationship

Write a LONG list of all the ways you know they love you, including small and big gestures.

Focus your attention on you and something you like to do.

Have a list of activities or friends and family you can call
– do this when a planned night or weekend doesn't
happen so you're not left with your own thoughts
swirling.

When you have jealous episodes, read the positive list,
especially the 'how you know they love you part' and do
an activity to take your mind off it. Jealousy is caused by
our thoughts and the good thing is that thoughts can be
changed with practice and determination.

5.   If you believe it is, then communicate

If you believe there is something they are doing wrong,
communicate your feelings to them in a non-obtrusive
way. Share your fears with your partner, explain how you
feel and seek their help in enabling you to overcome your
jealous emotions. Think of some things they can do to
make you feel more secure, whether it's to call more, take
an interest in your day, be more open with your thoughts

and ask them to do it. Don't forget to also ask them if there is anything you can do for them. Use this as an opportunity to strengthen your relationship/marriage and build a more solid foundation for the future. Communication is the foundation for marital success. If you can learn to communicate then you can express your emotions in a non-confrontational, non-accusatory, understanding and supportive environment.

Be careful not to blurt your fears out such as 'I think you are lying' or 'I think you are having an affair.' It might not be true and it will just add fuel to the fire. Explain that something seems to have changed in your relationship, explain what has changed and what makes you think your marriage is different. Be careful not to blame and don't get angry: just explain to your spouse what is going through your head and seek their help in trying to sort it out.

One of the most common relationship problems is expecting our partners to always know what we want and how we feel. But even with a ring on the finger, we aren't always mind readers, so if we haven't communicated our feelings and our partner doesn't know they have done something wrong, how do we expect them to do anything about it!

If any of this is resonating for you then tell them now and improve your communication and marriage. You have everything to gain and nothing to lose. Even if the answer isn't what you want to hear, knowledge is power and with knowledge comes the ability to turn your life around.

FEAR OF ABANDONMENT

Many people in this world have a fear of either being alone or being left alone by someone. There is an innate fear of living life without a partner and dealing with the world on your own. Throughout history, animals and humans have always had a partner to grow with and to build a family with. However, events throughout our lifetime, including our childhood, could contribute to this fear and even to the act of being abandoned. It is important to understand where these feelings and emotions are coming from, as well as to get the appropriate help to live a happy and healthy lifestyle along with a partner, if that is what you choose.

What Is A Fear of Abandonment And What Does It Mean?

Abandonment fear stems from thoughts and worries that involve a loved one leaving us. This can be caused by inadeQuate physical and emotional care throughout one's childhood. If you had a parent abandon your family when you were little, you saw first-hand the damage that abandonment can cause. It affects the entire family, mother, and children, and throws off the balance of the home. It can make it hard for that child to trust adults and it begins to manifest this fear of abandonment as they begin to worry who the next person to leave them will be.

If you are unable to form a trusting bond with someone, how will you know that they won't up and leave you? You may begin to feel as though you are incapable of being loved and this would then in turn negatively affect your self-esteem and self-image. Then, with low self-esteem coupled with a difficult childhood where whoever didn't meet your emotional needs abandoned you, you can develop this fear of abandonment and the fear that you are going to spend the rest of your life alone.

Where Does Fear Of Abandonment Come From?

As children, people may experience real losses, rejections or traumas that cause them to feel insecure and distrusting of the world. These losses and traumas can be dramatic, like the death of a loved one, neglect or emotional and physical abuse. However, they can also occur at a much subtler level, in everyday interactions between parents and children. In order to feel secure, children have to feel safe, seen, and soothed when they're upset. However, it's been said that even the best of parents are only fully attuned to their children around 30 percent of the time. Exploring their early attachment patterns can offer individuals insight into their fears around abandonment and rejection. Understanding how their parents related to them and whether they experienced a secure attachment versus an insecure one, can give people clues into how they view relationships in the present.

Secure attachments form when caretakers are consistently available and attuned to a child's needs. However, ruptures in these early relationships can lead children to form insecure attachments. From infancy, people learn to behave in ways that will best get their needs met by their parents or caretakers. A parent who may at one moment be present and meeting the child's needs, then at another moment be entirely unavailable and rejecting or, on the opposite end, intrusive and "emotionally hungry" can lead the child to form an ambivalent/ anxious attachment pattern. Children who experience this type of attachment tend to feel insecure. They may cling to the parent in an effort to get their needs met. However, they may also struggle to feel soothed by the parent. They are often anxious and unsure in relation to the parent, who is erratic in their behavior by sometimes being available and loving, and other times, rejecting or intrusive in ways that frustrate the child.

Fear of Abandonment: 10 Signs You Can't Ignore!

If you truly want to get to the root of your abandonment issues and come out all the better for it on the other side, there are a few key things that you're going to want to pay attention to moving forward.

1.   Long History With Abandonment Issues

Abandonment issues are caused by a wide variety of different reasons, but not all of them necessarily have to do with the choices you've made in the past. Many of them actually have to do with things that you were exposed to throughout your life. As a result, one of the major signs that you might have a fear of abandonment has to do with if any of the following apply to you:

•   Your parents got divorced, particularly at an early age.

•   You are a child of adopted parents.

- You are a child of alcoholic parents.

- You have a long history of low or non-existent self-esteem.

- Your caretakers, whoever they may have been, were emotionally unavailable.

- You were abused at some point during your childhood.

- You, unfortunately, lost a parent, a sibling or both.

All of these major factors are huge contributors to abandonment issues manifesting themselves later on in life.

2. You Can't (Or Won't) Commit

Another one of the major signs that you have abandonment issues takes the form of your commitment in relationships – or your lack thereof. Many people think that they're excellent romantic partners because they love the "newness" of a relationship. This is also commonly referred to as the "honeymoon period." Once that honeymoon is over, however, you tend to find reasons to end things almost immediately.

This isn't necessarily the sign of a string of bad luck – it's a sign that you have abandonment issues that you need to work on.

3.   Nobody Can Live Up to Your Standards

There's nothing wrong with trying to find perfection in a mate – so long as you don't let your expectations get too unrealistic. "Perfect for you" and "literally perfect" are two completely different things and should always be treated as such. Even people in the happiest, healthiest marriages that you could possibly find still have minor disagreements every now and again.

You should never let minor flaws cause you to break things off, which is exactly what fear of abandonment tends to do.

4. You Think Everyone Is Cheating On You

This is a particularly tricky topic, as it isn't necessarily found in something false. Infidelity is a very real thing, but if you constantly feel like EVERY romantic partner you have is cheating on you, you're probably dealing with something else entirely.

You have a fear of abandonment issues caused by low self-esteem. If you find your justification for your suspicions to be, "Of course this person is cheating on me – why would anyone not cheat on me?" then the problem doesn't rest with them at all. It rests with you.

5.   You Are Your Own Worst Enemy

Another one of the major signs that you have a fear of abandonment is when you can't seem to get out of your own way and let your relationship play out on its own. Just when things are going along really well, you have a tendency to screw things up.

Maybe you picked a fight over something small and insignificant. Maybe you did the unthinkable and actually cheated on your partner yourself.

This doesn't make you a bad person – this makes you someone with a solution in search of a problem that needs to be solved in the first place. You have the idea of "this is going to end poorly eventually, so I'm going to end it now on my own terms."

6.   You Can Be Very Controlling

Being a bit on the controlling side in a relationship is one thing – being excessively controlling to the point where you're essentially dictating how someone can live their life is something else entirely.

Irrationally questioning every small move a person makes isn't being in a relationship – it's being in a dictatorship. It's a major sign of mistrust on your part, which itself is one of the leading signs that you have a deeply rooted fear of abandonment that it is no longer healthy for you to ignore.

7.   You Are Often Negative

Another one of the major signs that you have a fear of abandonment actually begins alongside the relationship itself. You meet a great new guy or girl who seems interested, but you can't help but immediately noticing flaws.

Some of them are small – he or she has an irritating voice or likes a movie that you think is awful. Sometimes they're big – you don't like what they do as a job or they have opinions that you very much disagree with.

The problem is that you're letting them act as barriers that will prevent you from getting more serious with the other person. This all falls back on the idea that you fear getting hurt so badly that you create these artificial "faults" to stay ahead of the game.

This is also related to the unrealistic expectations that you tend to set for potential mates, otherwise known as the "Prince Charming" fantasy.

8. You Become Far Too Attached Far Too Quickly

One of the major signs that you have a fear of abandonment is if you instantly fall head over heels with whoever you meet. As soon as you meet someone, you're "in it for the long haul," even if you haven't really gotten a chance to know each other in the first place.

This isn't "love at first sight" – this is clinginess, which is one of the major ways that people with abandonment issues tend to sabotage themselves.

In your own head, not only do you get to avoid abandonment by eventually being the one to do the abandoning, but you also create your own "get out of jail free" card. "I didn't do anything wrong," you say to yourself. "I was in this 100% from the start."

In reality, all you've done is found another effective way to end your romantic chances before they really had a chance to get off the ground in the first place.

9. You NEVER Allow Yourself to Attach

Unfortunately, the opposite end of the spectrum is also true. If you absolutely NEVER allow yourself to get attached to a relationship, regardless of how perfect the other person may seem, you're looking at another in a long series of abandonment issues that you would do well to address for the sake of everyone involved.

You may tell yourself that you don't want to get too serious too quickly. You may tell yourself that you value your single lifestyle and don't want to commit before you're ready. What you're really doing is being emotionally uninvested, which is absolutely NOT how a healthy relationship is formed.

10.   Your Fear of Abandonment Isn't Just Linked to Your Romantic Life

Finally, if you really want to identify signs of abandonment issues, look outside of your romantic pursuits. Say you're unhappy with your job and really want to make a change, yet you never quite make the effort to polish that resume because the "interview process is a hassle."

Maybe that's true or maybe you don't want to apply for a job because you don't want to be rejected.

Maybe you're creative and you've just had an idea for a great short story. You never get down to putting pen to paper, however, because you're afraid people won't like it. "It's better if it just lives inside my head," you think. "It's easier that way."

Or, you don't want to face the potential rejection along the road to getting that story published.

The fact of the matter is that a fear of abandonment very rarely exists in a silo. It doesn't JUST affect one area of your life (like your romantic life) while leaving other areas unscathed. It tends to affect EVERYTHING about the life you're living, often negatively.

If you start looking outside of your romantic relationships and see signs of abandonment and rejection issues, guess what – it just might explain a thing or two about your ex-girlfriends or ex-boyfriends, too.

Again – absolutely none of this is to say that you are incapable of love or that you're in some way "broken." If you are, everyone else is too. What this means is that you are aware of the artificial barriers that you're creating for yourself, particularly when it comes to your romantic pursuits.

If the first step to recovery is admitting we have a problem, a simple acknowledgment of these warning signs puts you in the best possible position to actually do something about them moving forward.

How Will This Fear Impact My Relationships?

One may think that this fear would leave once becoming involved in a committed relationship. However, this is not usually the case. Those fears can manifest themselves in ways where the person firmly believes that their partner will leave them and that it is just a matter of when, not if. So, they live each day worrying about being abandoned and not being able to give all of themselves to their relationship. They accuse their partners of cheating or making attempts to leave them.

They firmly believe that their partner is just waiting for the moment to walk away from their relationship. They feel as though they are unable to trust their partner's word, as their trust was broken by others in the past. However, what this does is create a rift between them and their partner and will make their self-fulfilling prophecy come true because by living as though their relationship is ending the day in and day out, they end their relationship.

However, they do not blame themselves and usually do not see how they contributed to their relationship's ultimate demise. They just simply believe that they are "doomed" in a relationship, they are "unlovable" and that everyone in their life leaves them without explanation. Therefore, without having this insight, the issues at hand will not be rectified and they will move onto the next relationship and continue these struggles.

Can This Affect Other Relationships?

The answer is yes. Most people who have a fear of abandonment do not only have this fear with a romantic partner. Instead, this could be with their parents, friends, and children. Usually, these fears manifest themselves throughout a person's childhood. Oftentimes, there is a parent who is absent from the home or may leave home suddenly and without warning. When this occurs, that child feels abandoned by their parent. However, if this parent also comes and goes throughout the child's life, they may be fearful to trust that their parent is going to stay around, as when they begin to believe that they are staying, they leave again.

Fast forward a few years to teenagers, and then you have someone who has the potential to be a very clingy friend. They may want to always be around their friends and get upset if their friend makes a new friend for fear that they will be left behind. Now, if their friend knows their family history, they may understand this clinginess, but it may also become annoying. If that is the case, they may cease the friendship. That would then become a loss and, to that teenager, show that someone else just up and left them. Without having the insight into how they contributed to that, the cycle will continue.

Now into their adulthood, they are in and out of relationships on this very issue. They become involved with a person, whom they have difficulty trusting and whom they think will abandon them. Therefore, they are afraid to get close to them, and they are afraid to love them. Without being able to reciprocate feelings, their partner leaves. They continue to not take responsibility for the downfall of another relationship and the cycle continues.

Unfortunately, this can continue for all relationships in a person's life until they can finally realize that they may be contributing to this cycle of "everyone" leaving them throughout their lives. True, they could not control the behaviors of their parent, but recognizing that is where these feelings began and that they do not need to continue is key. Once this is realized, then the rebuilding can begin, and they can live a happy and healthy life with a life-long partner.

Effect on Relationships: An Example Scenario

The fear of abandonment is highly personalized. Some people are solely afraid of losing a romantic partner and others fear suddenly finding themselves completely alone.

To better explain how individuals with a fear of abandonment may navigate a relationship, here is an example of how a typical relationship may start and evolve. It is especially true for romantic relationships, but there are many similarities in close friendships as well:

1.   Getting to Know One Another Phase

At this point, you feel relatively safe. You are not yet emotionally invested in the other person, so you continue to live your life while enjoying time with your chosen person.

2.   The Honeymoon Phase

This is when you make the choice to commit. You are willing to overlook possible red or yellow flags because you just get along so well. You start spending a great deal of time with the other person, you always enjoy yourself, and you start to feel secure.

3.   The Real Relationship

The honeymoon phase cannot last forever. No matter how well two people get along, real life always intervenes. People get sick, have family problems, start working difficult hours, worry about money, and need time to get things done.

Although this is a very normal and positive step in a relationship, it can be terrifying for those with a fear of abandonment who may see it as a sign that the other person is pulling away.

If you have this fear, you are probably battling with yourself and trying very hard not to express your worries for fear of appearing clingy.

4.   The Slight

People are human. They have foibles and moods and things on their minds. Regardless of how much they care for someone else, they cannot and should not be expected to always have that person at the forefront of their minds. Especially once the honeymoon period is over, it is inevitable that a seeming slight will occur. This often takes the form of an unanswered text message, an unreturned phone call or a request for a few days of alone time.

5. The Reaction

For those with a fear of abandonment, this is a turning point. If you have this fear, you are probably completely convinced that the slight is a sign that your partner no longer loves you. What happens next is almost entirely determined by the fear of abandonment, its severity, and the sufferer's preferred coping style.

Some people handle this by becoming clingy and demanding, insisting that their partner prove her love by jumping through hoops. Others run away, rejecting their partners before they are rejected. There are others who feel that the slight is their fault and attempt to transform themselves into the "perfect partner" in a quest to keep the other person from leaving.

In reality, the slight is most likely not a slight at all. Simply put, sometimes people just do things that their partners do not understand. In a healthy relationship, the partner may recognize the situation for what it is—a normal reaction that has little or nothing to do with the relationship. Or he may feel upset by it, but address it with either a calm discussion or a brief argument. Either way, a single perceived slight does not become a dominating influence on the partner's feelings.

6. The Partner's Point of View

From your partner's point of view, your sudden personality shift seems to come from out of left field. If your partner does not suffer from a fear of abandonment, he probably does not have the slightest idea as to why his previously confident, laid-back partner is suddenly acting clingy and demanding, smothering him with attention or pulling away altogether.

Similar to phobias, it is impossible to simply talk or reason someone out of a fear of abandonment. No matter how many times your partner tries to reassure you, it will simply not be enough. Eventually, your behavior patterns and inconsolable reactions could drive your partner away, leading to the very conclusion that you fear most.

Coping Strategies

If your fear is mild and well-controlled, you may be able to get a handle on it simply by becoming educated about your tendencies and learning new behavior strategies. For most people, though, the fear of abandonment is rooted in deep-seated issues that are difficult to unravel alone.

Although treating the fear itself is critical, it is also essential to build a feeling of belonging. Rather than focusing all of your energy and devotion on a single partner, focus on building a community. No one person can solve all of our problems or meet all of our needs. But a solid group of several close friends can each play an important role in our lives.

Many people with a fear of abandonment state that they never felt like they had a "tribe" or a "pack" when they were growing up. For whatever reasons, they always felt like the "other" or disconnected from those around them. But the good news is that it's never too late.

Whatever your current stage of life, it is important to surround yourself with other like-minded individuals. Make a list of your current hobbies, passions, and dreams. Then find others who share your interests. While it is true that not everyone who shares an interest will become a close friend, hobbies and dreams are an excellent stepping stone toward building a solid support network. Working on your passions also helps build self-confidence and the belief that you are strong enough to cope with whatever life throws your way.

How Can I Have A Lasting Relationship?

The very first step towards enjoying life with someone is to be able to squash that fear. Now, that is very much so easier said than done. However, it must be done one way or another. You need to rebuild your confidence, both in yourself and in your relationships. You need to be able to understand that you are, in fact, lovable and worthy of love. By improving your self-esteem, you will learn to understand that you do deserve love and you need to find someone that is worthy of your love. Only by doing so will you be able to feel as though you should be in a committed relationship, as this may not be something that you can do on your own. Through BetterHelp, you can access virtual licensed therapists who are available to provide online counseling about this very topic. Online counseling is completely professional and private but provides full therapy sessions from the comfort of your own home.

The next step is extremely hard. You need to be able to trust. Now, for some people, this is a humongous struggle, especially if they have trusted people in the past who have betrayed that trust. However, each new person in our lives is worth a new effort. We cannot punish them for mistakes that someone else made. Instead of living each day waiting for them to leave you, put forth all the effort possible to try to keep them in your life. Now, if the relationship is struggling, this is not to say to put up with any actions that are abusive or that make you feel uncomfortable, but rather do not set your relationship up for failure before it truly had the chance to begin. As mentioned above, utilizing licensed therapists is an ideal way to address these issues. The therapy can be both one-on-one with a therapist, as well as couples counseling to build upon your relationship.

Am I Doomed?

Of course not! The very best thing about life is that at any given moment, the human being can change. They can say, "I've had about enough of this," and make a concerted effort to change their lives. Without support and guidance of a professional, this can happen. It will not be easy, and it will take a lot of work, but in the end, you will feel like a whole new person.

Once you can let go of that fear, you will feel as though a huge weight has been lifted off of your chest. You will have a new lease on life and will be seeking those relationships that you would like to last a lifetime. The difference is, then you will wholeheartedly believe that you deserve that love and you will be able to work towards your relationship's survival, rather than sabotaging it with your negative fears.

Remember, there are people in your life that love and care about you. And again, you can utilize the help right here at BetterHelp, as well as any licensed therapist, to build yourself back up again. Fears can be debilitating, but overcoming these fears can be an exhilarating feeling and is so worth it in the long run.

Strategies To Calm Down When You Experience Fear Of Abandonment

Every one of us has fears about being left alone. Most of us struggle with some fundamental feelings that we are unlovable or won't be accepted for who we are. We all have a "critical inner voice," a negative internal dialogue that chronically criticizes us or gives us bad advice. This 'voice' often perpetuates our fear of abandonment: "He's gonna leave you," it warns. "She's probably cheating," it cries. Because we all have "voices" and alarms that are set off when we feel triggered, it's helpful to have tools and strategies to calm ourselves down when we notice our fears amp up. One useful resource is this toolkit to help

105

people cope with anxiety, which lists exercises and practices that are beneficial for anyone to utilize when they feel stirred up.

Another general practice to adopt is that of self-compassion. Researcher Dr. Kristin Neff has done studies, revealing countless benefits of self-compassion. Enhancing self-compassion is actually favorable to building self-esteem because self-compassion doesn't focus as much on judgment and evaluation. Rather, it involves three main elements:

Self-kindness - This refers to the idea that people should be kind, as opposed to judgmental, toward themselves. This sounds simple in theory but is much more difficult in practice. The more people can have a warm, accepting attitude toward themselves and their struggles, the stronger they'll feel in the face of difficult circumstances. We can all be a better friend to ourselves, even if we feel hurt or abandoned by someone else.

Mindfulness - Being mindful is helpful because it helps people not to over-identify with their thoughts and feelings in ways that allow them to get carried away. When people feel afraid of something like being abandoned, they tend to have a lot of mean thoughts toward themselves, thus perpetuating this fear. Imagine if you could acknowledge these thoughts and feelings without letting them overtake you. Could you take a gentler attitude toward yourself and let these thoughts pass like clouds in the sky instead of floating off with them – without losing your sense of yourself and, often, reality?

Common humanity - The more each of us can accept that we are human and, like all humans, we will struggle in our lives, the more self-compassion and strength we can cultivate. If individuals can consistently remember that they are not alone and that they are worthy, they can help themselves avoid believing those cruel and incorrect messages telling them that they will be abandoned or that they're unwanted.

Moving On From Fear Of Abandonment

Fear of abandonment can feel very real and very painful, but if people can practice self-compassion, they are more likely to get through those times when they're triggered. The more individuals can trace these feelings to their roots in their past, the more they can separate these experiences from the present. It takes courage for someone to be willing to see what hurt them and face the primal feelings of abandonment they may have had as children when they had no control over their situation. However, when people are able to face these feelings, they can essentially set themselves free from many of the chains of their past. They can become differentiated adults, who are able to create new stories and new relationships in which they feel safe, seen, soothed, and secure.

Did you like this book, or did you find it useful, until now?

Your support really makes a difference! I would be very grateful if you would publish an exhaustive review on **Amazon.** *All reviews are read personally so that I can get real feedback and make this book (and the whole series) even better.*

Thanks again for your support!

CONFLICT IN RELATIONSHIPS

Conflict in relationships occurs from time to time. Though this happens in all relationships, it becomes a serious issue, especially in a marital relationship. One thing that comes in the way of a conflict getting resolved is arguments. Arguments between a married couple is so common that it is considered a natural thing to occur. But the potential of an argument for destruction is very great. Unfortunately, many people do not understand the serious damage arguments can do to a relationship.

An interesting thing about arguments is that each of the two partners listens to the other's argument. This active listening is in sharp contrast to the commonly expressed grievance by many people that their spouses don't listen to them. So, it turns out that your spouse does not listen to you in the normal course but will listen to you keenly when you start arguing! Unfortunately, this active listening becomes even more harmful than the failure to listen to a spouse, in general. This is because of the special effect an argument produces.

Conflict in relationships can, in many cases, be resolved by each of the partners discussing the issues openly. But let us see what happens when one starts arguing. The moment one person starts arguing, a small structure called Amygdala located at the top of the brain stem gets activated and takes control. When Amygdala takes control, it seeks to interpret a situation as good, bad or dangerous and the brain acts on this interpretation. It is responsible for emotional memory and scientific research has concluded that Amygdala triggers two emotions - rage and fear. The Amygdala circuit also transmits information twice as fast as the neocortex, which is the thinking part of the brain. The panic triggered by the Amygdala takes effect before rational thinking gets a chance to have a say.

When rage and fear become the dominant emotions, the person starts exploding, losing control over what he or she says or does. The result is, aggravation of the situation beyond repair. If you are at the receiving end of a bitter argument, Amygdala takes over and within a fraction of a second, your face will turn red and your heart will seem to be on the verge of leaping out of your chest.

Unfortunately, our brain's architecture favors emotion over rationality. However, it is within our control to avoid situations leading to bitter arguments. Though many of us might have experienced that making up after a bitter argument does not fully erase the bitterness created by the argument, we may not be aware why this is so.

What No One Told You About Conflicts in Relationships

Many people lack a real in-depth understanding of what conflict really says about a person and conversely, they mistakenly believe that when conflicts arise they are merely the result of two or more people who disagree about a particular issue. In reality, the causes of conflict go much deeper and are rooted in our own feelings of emotional security or lack thereof, which is a product of the conditioning we receive from an early age to hide our true selves out of a fear of rejection. When you add these two factors together, the result is an internal contradiction in how we should communicate and we are prevented from expressing ourselves openly and honestly while also being mindful of how we deliver our message.

So instead, we hide behind polite responses, agree simply for the sake of peacekeeping or refrain from expressing our true feelings which only keeps the conflicts we ignore active within ourselves. Doing this leaves these issues

113

bubbling just below the surface, ready and waiting to be triggered by the next event that pushes our 'hot button.'

As children, we are taught to regulate our behavior in socially acceptable ways. We are told that big boys and girls don't cry and that we should not say things that will make others feel bad. While it is true that we must be sensitive to the feelings and opinions of others, there is a measurable difference between social etiquette and diplomacy and being unable to express our thoughts and feelings. This inability to communicate effectively can only be traced back to our early programming and the deficit it creates in the conflict management skills department.

It is unfortunate that, in spite of our incredible technological and scientific advances, we are still willing to accept such inadequate communication and problem-solving skills as just another part of life despite the evidence that doing so does not serve our needs or interests or anyone else's. Instead, our tendency is to utilize the same conditioned responses to conflict, expect different results and become more unbalanced when our conflicts are not resolved – which, according to any dictionary, is the true definition of insanity!

If we want to avoid being victims of conflict and resolve them when they arise in our daily lives, it requires that we take a deeper look into ourselves, our programming and our tolerances. We must be willing to let go of our preconditioned responses which in turn will alter our behaviors and our reactions.

When conflict is responded to with more conflict, the cycle perpetuates and the gap between the disputants continues to widen. Why? Because as I stated earlier: All unresolved conflicts lie just below the surface. Whenever a conflict arises, it doesn't matter whether the disagreement at that moment involves the same person or issue from the last conflict we encountered, our defensive button has been pushed and the situation at hand likely deteriorates. This true inner working of conflict may be unlike any other explanation you may be familiar with, but it speaks to the true nature of conflict, why it continues, how it can escalate and the damage it causes to relationships. What is important to understand is that if conflicts are not resolved in a manner that is acceptable to the individuals involved, whether through compromise, agreeing to disagree or involving a neutral third party to inject another point of view, there will be no closure. This is how the cycle continues.

If you have ever had a disagreement with someone and out of nowhere they begin to pull in issues that happened a month, a year or even three years ago, you are witnessing their unresolved inner conflict and the lack of personal power and control the other person is experiencing within themselves. Suppressed conflicts are always looking for outward expression and quite often it doesn't really matter how or when they come out. This is why responding to conflict with more conflict cannot only be dangerous, it also won't resolve anything. So if you are confronted with conflict, does that mean that you should not defend your views or position? No, it means that you must be aware of your own feelings and responses. The caveat here is that there is a bit of an art to disarming and resolving conflict which lies in actively listening to what is really being conveyed, not what you think you are hearing and, this is the important part, controlling your tendency to react or respond defensively, which will only escalate the problem. The more effective approaches are to revisit the situation when everyone is in a calmer state of mind or agree to discuss the situation with neither person assigning blame nor punishment to the other. And yes, this does take personal discipline, self-control, and some practice at first, but over time not only will conflicts lose their emotional charge over you, you will find that you are able to see them coming and take steps to avoid playing a role in perpetuating the vicious cycle.

Relationships and The Role of Mutual Blame

"It's all your fault that I drink."

This is just an example of how people in relationships blame one another. I am sure the reader can come up with many more from their own relationships. What is important to understand about mutual blame is that it never works. It is usually in the context of the arguments that a couple starts to engage in the process of mutual blame. Once that happens, the couple starts to become defensive and angrier than at the start. Being told you are to blame for something is being told you are incompetent, at fault and lacking in many ways. No one wants to feel backed into a corner and forced to confess to being wrong. Because one's pride and ego become involved, it becomes necessary to prove the other person wrong and to then blame them. In fact, even knowing that they are to blame for something, a partner will deny they are responsible.

The nature of relationships is such that everyone is at fault because everyone contributes, in some way, to the problem. In other words, people in a relationship impact one another in many ways. The fact that they impact one another provides a good and convenient reason to engage in blame. In reality, it is rare that anyone is totally to blame for many of the things that happen. Relating means that there are interactions going on between two people who have a history and future together. Interaction does not mean that one partner caused something to happen to the other. Each individual is responsible for their own behaviors, separate and apart from the other. For example, if I had a bad day, it does not mean that my partner caused it. Another example might be that "I withdraw from interacting because of your criticisms" which really means that "I feel like I want to withdraw when I hear criticism." An age-old example is that "you gave me a headache." In reality, "I have a headache." Why blame it on another person?

In the end, it is better when in a conflict, to find ways to find solutions to the disagreement. Sometimes it is as simple as finding a better way to phrase things. Communication is more than one individual speaking. Rather, communication means listening first and then responding in non-defensive ways. For example, using the pronoun "I" when speaking is far better than an accusatory "you." Also, the use of the word "why" as in "why do you" is accusatory. It sounds a lot better to say, "I am so angry that I got laid off that I want to blame everyone." Another example is to say, "I wish we could find a solution that you would find acceptable." The choice of words is always important.

In a permanent relationship, the goal should not be to win an argument at the expense of the other person, not if you value that person. In close relations, winning an argument can mean losing the relationship.

Rather than blame, find solutions.

How to Resolve a Relationship Conflict Effectively

Every relationship has conflict. You simply can't put two human beings together for an extended period of time, let alone several years, and never have any conflict develop. Unfortunately, many couples simply don't know how to handle conflict and resolve it effectively when it does occur. Without those skills, your relationship is going to continue being a struggle for both of you.

Unresolved conflict is like a cut on your finger that becomes infected. Even if it starts out very small, it can quickly become very painful and cause a lot of distress. Cleaning out the wound may be painful initially, but it is necessary if the wound is ever going to heal.

Unresolved conflict is very destructive and may ultimately destroy your relationship. But if you learn to make a few changes in your approach, you will resolve conflict in your relationship much more quickly and smoothly.

Keep in mind that if you are fighting, you must fight fair. Fighting dirty is akin to sucker punching your partner. It's going to make him angry and he may retaliate (or withdraw) in response. If it's difficult for the two of you to talk without it escalating to a fight, set some ground rules to which you both must agree. Then stick to them! It won't be easy, but it will make a world of difference in your relationship!

Here are some guidelines to help you:

• **Stay calm. ALWAYS.** This is not going to be easy but is one of the most important things you can do when trying to resolve a conflict that is plaguing your relationship. When your partner is hurtful or angry, if you stay calm, you may disarm him and he will be more likely to retreat. It will also help keep your conversation from escalating (because it takes two for that to happen!).

- **Really listen to what your partner is saying, as well as what he is communicating non-verbally as well.** If he is particularly angry, chances are he just really wants you to hear him. If you haven't done that in the past, now is the time to start. Let him finish before you respond. Truly listening is a way of showing both courtesy and respect. You may have been impatient to respond or defensive and reactive - waiting to jump in rather than really paying attention.

- **Never interrupt or attempt to talk over your partner.** This is a great way to infuriate him, as it is very disrespectful and clearly conveys the message you think your words are more important than his. Also, it is very rude behavior.

- **Don't dredge up past hurts or wrongs.** Leave the past in the past. Bringing it up again is never productive and will only widen the rift between you. It also gives the impression that you are keeping score and it will almost inevitably put your partner on the defensive.

• **Work out your conflicts in private**. When you confront your partner or try to discuss relationship matters, doing it when others are around will not only be very uncomfortable, it may make your partner feel like you've set him up. Give both your partner and others the courtesy of keeping these matters between the two of you.

• **Don't engage in childish fighting.** Name calling, bullying or pulling in friends to take your side, for example, are behaviors that at best belong on a grade school playground, not in an adult relationship.

•   **Take ownership of your role in the conflict.** Blaming everything on your partner will get you nowhere (except perhaps alone).

•   **Don't take the stance that your partner is wrong and you are right.** Being right is highly overrated, and the need to always be right will make you a very undesirable relationship partner. Strive for understanding, mutual resolution, and kindness instead.

•   **Always try to find the grain of truth (even if it seems very tiny) in anything your partner says.** He most likely is not totally to be blamem, and therefore probably has some valid points. Listen for them and acknowledge your agreement.

•   **Don't use extreme words such as "always" or "never" to describe any of your partner's behaviors.**

Not only are these highly unlikely to be true, they will tap into your partner's desire to stop opening up.

It takes two to tango and you both need to take ownership of your part in the conflict.

If you are serious about saving your marriage, you may want to discuss these guidelines with your partner and ask him if he agrees that they are reasonable. If he does, ask him if he will commit to following them whenever you have a potentially heated conversation.

THE LIFE CYCLE OF RELATIONSHIPS

If you are in a relationship that seems to be headed towards commitment such as getting engaged, married, having kids, etc., it may be a good idea to familiarize yourself with the relationship lifecycle. There are five stages to all relationships. Couples move through the various stages at different speeds, will move back and forth from stage to stage and at times, will find themselves in the same stage and other times in different state. Understanding the stages helps the couple normalize what they are experiencing and make better decisions.

1.   Romance Stage

All relationships begin with this stage. The need satisfied here is love and belonging. This stage is characterized by its dream-like qualities, fantasies, and hopes for the future. The role of this stage is to give the couple a taste of the potential of their union and it lasts anywhere between 2 months to 2 years but averages 6 months. When a person is in this stage, their body produces vast amounts of endorphins, which makes them feel unusually happy, positive and excited about everything in their life. There is not much to fix at this point and the couples are encouraged to continue to explore one another.

2. Power Struggle Stage

During the exploration process, differences are discovered and power struggle sets in. This is the most difficult of all stages and is usually the time when relationships terminate. As couples become emotionally and physically more intimate, weaknesses and vulnerabilities begin to surface and conflicts ensue.

The need satisfied now is power and some freedom. The role of this stage is to make each individual gain awareness of themselves and their partner and to begin to relate to each other as whole people. Power struggle starts soon after the two move in together and can last for many bitter years. During this stage, a couple has three options: terminate, continue to stay together but live parallel lives, or learn how to fight fairly with both winning and declaring one's own individuality.

3.   Stability Stage

If as a child one did not learn coping skills, then the power struggle phase was exceptionally hard. However, upon survival, the couple becomes okay with each other's differences and establishes clear boundaries. The need satisfied in this stage is freedom and choice.

The danger at this stage is that the couple may start to realize that each other's paths in life may be different. There is a sense of loss and sadness as dreams do not materialize. There may be a feeling of boredom, a sense of not being connected and having nothing in common.

The focus is on the present, not the future because that is still undecided.

This is the second most common stage for counseling or divorce. In the beginning, it feels good to agree to stop changing the other, but life is all about growth and change. At this stage, the couple has history and should use it as an advantage to persevere in the relationship. At this point, mutual respect sets in or the couple revert to a power struggle.

4.   Commitment Stage

This is the stage when the couple should contemplate marriage. Unfortunately, people usually have already married in the romance stage. That's unfortunate because when they reach the power struggle stage, they wonder what hit them. In this stage, the couple is making clear choices about themselves and their partner, based both on differences and commonalities.

The needs fulfilled here are a balance of love, belonging, fun, power, and freedom. This is a stage when two individuals realize they don't need to be with each other but choose to be. Overall, this is the stage when the couple finally begins to feel comfortable and happy with their deepening consistent relationship. Some people feel a sense of loss in this stage as they learn to accept their partner for who they truly are since this means they have to let go of the fantasy of who they want their partner to be. At this phase, individuals begin to re-establish their own outside interests and friendships, which were given up in the Romance Phase. There is some danger that the couple may begin to drift apart or become bored with each other. The remedy is to try to maintain the connection that was created in the Romance Phase by establishing date night, flirting and making each other a priority.

5.   Co-creation Stage

In this stage, the couple have decided to be a team moving out into the world. This world may include children, a project, a joint business venture, etc. The role of this stage is to handle any common project or life crisis as a perfect team, acting as one: proactively, responsibly, and constructively to a mutual fulfillment. The danger at this stage is over involvement with the outside world and relationship being neglected. The relationship must be continually nurtured along the way. There needs to be time for you, for me, for us and for them. This is difficult sometimes and choices must be made.

What to Do If You Are Losing Interest in Your Partner

When you first met, everything was exciting and new - it was like you were embarking on a great adventure. You got to know each other some more and you started to get used to each other. After a while, it was no longer exciting and new. It was just the two of you and now you've noticed a problem, which is that you are losing interest in your partner. Now, this doesn't have to mean doom and gloom, but it does depend on what stage your relationship is at.

If your relationship is fairly new, then the simple reason that you are losing interest in your partner is that you just don't love them. That's no one's fault. If your partner just isn't your type then it is not worth continuing and building a relationship in which you'll both be unhappy. On the other hand, if your relationship is more established, it's a little bit more serious but the chances are that you have both let your relationship grow stale so you should be able to resolve the problem.

The first thing that you need to do is to ask yourself why you are losing interest in your partner. Are there any specific reasons or is it just a general lack of interest? If there are specific issues then you need to talk to your partner about them and find a way forward from there. It could be a case that your partner is having problems which they didn't want to burden you with, and trying to deal with those problems has somehow changed them. If it's just a general 'not interested' then you need to look at re-invigorating the relationship and your life.

We all have our wants and needs and we use a variety of sources to fulfill them. We all have our own lives, histories, friends, hobbies, opinions and what have you which make us who you are. Your problem could be that you have made your partner your sole source for fulfilling your needs, and if they cannot do everything for you then it is only natural that you start to lose interest in them. Even though you are in a relationship, you still need to have your own space in order to maintain a sense of who you are. If you lose who you are then you are no longer the person that your partner fell in love with. Go out with your friends and pursue your own hobbies and interests as it helps you to not only grow as a person but to bring new ideas and experiences (and gossip) to your relationship.

How much time do you actually spend in talking to each other? The thing about communication is that it binds you together and it makes you a part of each other's lives. When you stop communicating then how can you connect with each other, how can you share your emotions, how can you know when your partner needs you? If you don't communicate with each other, then your relationship will become boring, which could be why you are losing interest in your partner.

Do you spend quality time together or do you just come home from work and watch the T.V? I know that we all have such busy lives, but when you stop making time for each other, it can become habit-forming, and then it becomes too much effort. You need that time together to become closer and to be able to relax from the stresses and strains of everyday life. It doesn't have to be something extravagant, maybe something as simple as meeting for lunch in a park or just going for a coffee. The vital thing is that you are doing something together that you enjoy. If you are bored with doing the same thing time and time again, then find something new to do, new things to see, new places to visit, find new things to excite and stimulate your relationship.

And do you still connect with each other, do you know if your partner has any feelings for you, do they know if you have any feelings for them? If you love someone, then tell them. Otherwise, how will they know? We need people to tell us that they love us, not just once in a while but everyday. It does not take a lot of effort to hug or kiss your partner and tell them that you love them, and it means so much as well. Unleash the romantic in you and do things for your partner to make them happy, which also has the side benefit of making you happy as well. Leave notes for your partner to find, call, text or email them and tell them how much they mean to you. If you both start doing that again then you should hopefully not just stop losing interest in your partner, but regain an active interest in them.

What to do if you are losing interest in your partner? If it's early in your relationship, it could mean that they're not for you. If your relationship is more developed, then start working on your relationship again: relationships don't just happen of their own accord, you have to work at them. Add some life to your relationship and reconnect with each other. Spend time together, talk, and plan for the future. If you are having problems then you need to talk them through with your partner as they will probably have noticed that something is wrong. If you both want to make the relationship work, then commit to doing what you can to create the best possible relationship that you can, you might even surprise yourself.

The Incredible Ways To Reconnect With Your Partner

When you start to notice that you haven't been as close as you once were with your partner, you will want to start taking steps that will reconnect you with your partner and re-establish the strong relationship that you once had.

- **Realize that the mess can wait**

Some women believe that they are being constantly judged by how their house or their living space looks. However, this is far from the case. Instead of making cleaning the majority of your free time, why not allow yourself to let more things go at the end of the day to make room for your relationship? Instead of having the laundry always done and the kitchen always shining, isn't your relationship worth the time?

- **Take time for yourself**

Many women will feel more connected in their relationships if they take the time to make themselves look good. Something as simple as getting out of sweatpants and t-shirts at the end of the day and into nice jeans and a well-fitting top can help you feel more confident and thus, more attractive to your partner. You don't have to look like a model, but taking care of your appearance can help you feel like one.

- **Create a date**

At least once a week, you and your partner need to get out of the house and on a date. Too often, long relationships think that they are 'past' that, so they settle into a dull life of staying at home. When you were first dating, you went to the movies and out to eat – why not try to do that more now? Sure, you won't be able to do it every week, but if you try, you will both have something to look forward to.

- **Stop your thinking**

Many times, a woman can become frustrated by everything that she is handling, especially when she's a mom as well as a career woman. When this happens, you might feel as though you could scream at your partner for not being helpful enough, romantic enough, etc. But is this really going to reconnect your relationship? It can help to stop your thinking for a few seconds before you share these kinds of feelings. You might find that you're actually feeling something else that's not directed at him.

- **Put the spotlight on him**

When you take the time to do something special for someone else, you will reap the benefits of feeling closer to them as well. Something as simple as packing a lunch or writing a love note in their wallet can be a great way to help your partner know that you care. Everyone likes to feel special.

- **When you can't get away**

It's time to be creative if you're unable to get away from the house. Maybe you can create date night at home or work together on some goals that you've wanted to accomplish. Play board games – do whatever you both like to do together. If you have a home remodeling project, don't leave it just for him - do it together to get more couple time.

- **Getting out of town**

One of the best ways to reconnect as a couple is to head out of the house for a few days. There are numerous bed and breakfasts that you can visit for only a small expense. You don't even have to leave the room if you don't want to, but the time away from your normal distractions can help you get back in tune with what your relationship needs.

Be the Person Your Partner Wants to Date

In relationships and of course marriages, we might love our partner but sometimes we may not like them very much. Sure, we can be mad and know we still love them but given the choice, are they someone we would want to date? Are you someone they would date? Oh my gosh, are you someone you would date?

Many couples come into my office and say their main issue is of course communication. "We don't communicate." I hear that over and over. It is true too. Of course, they use words and actions to communicate, so it would seem as though it should not be so hard. Yet, it is hard. What is really going on is that, at a deeper level, they do not believe the other person actually understands them. When we do not sense that feeling of being understood, typically our response will be to repeat ourselves in vain, leading to emotions such as frustration and anger when we cannot get to feeling understood. It is as though our partner is unavailable to us. We may react to those emotions by escalating the situation with that anger or perhaps instead we shut down and become distant. Sound ripe for a big fight? Fortunately, these arguments are completely avoidable with a few simple rules of engagement.

First, let's talk about dating. When we go out on a date, usually it signals that we like or are open to liking the other person. When you are going out on a date, I think it is safe to say that we hold an expectation that the other person will make an effort to be kind, considerate, polite, and respectful in our presence, and we plan to do the same. If they are not these things, we probably will not want to go out with them again. Would you ever want to date someone who was rude, inconsiderate and contemptuous? Do you already? Are you married to them?

What if you are the one who is rude, inconsiderate and contemptuous? Be honest. If you really dislike your partner and are unwilling to be a nice person to be around, then why are you in the relationship? You are torturing them and probably living an unhappy life. On the other hand, and hopefully, if you are willing to put in the effort to build or rebuild your relationship, here are a few basic things you can do right now to help the relationship feel better quickly.

1.   Be Present with Them

If your partner is talking to you, it is important for you to actually pay attention. This is the one people blow all the time. When they are talking, are you texting, looking at email, half watching television? If so, you are not fully present and they feel it. Soon they will either get angry at you or quit trying.

How do you communicate that you are listening and are interested? Hold eye contact, nod your head and say things like, "Uh huh," "Okay," or "No kidding." Have you ever tried to share something important with someone who had a blank face and did not give you cues that they were listening and interested? How did that go for you? Also, know it is okay to ask questions to help you understand. That is participation.

Now, I know what you are thinking. No, this does not mean you have to drop everything anytime they start talking. Yet, there are some critical moments to do this. Moments of reconnection, when one or both of you return from work, is one. Whoever comes home goes and finds the other person, greets them ideally with a hug, and you talk for 10 to 15 minutes to connect with each other. This is the time to be fully present and share. The other time to tune in is when your partner clearly wants or needs to have a conversation about something important to them. If you are often distracted, you are communicating, "You are not important enough for me to stop and listen." Trust me, communicating that will not go well for you in the long run.

2. Listen Without Interrupting

One reason people interrupt is to clarify something the other person said. Avoid this; it is merely a fantasy. Everyone has their own story, their own truth. Sure, it is great to try and reconcile your experience with your partner, and if you can do it gently, it will work sometimes. However, I am willing to wager that the facts you are trying to correct will sidetrack your partner way from their real intentions behind sharing their story. It will also block them from getting their need for feeling understood and being important met. Correcting them will both sidetrack their story and leave them feeling dismissed. In response, you will either get a bunch of charged energy that looks like anger or they will shut down and give up.

3. Do not try to "fix it"

Guess what: I will venture to say that out of 100 times your partner is sharing something, maybe in ninety-eight of those times they just want you to listen with compassion and concern. I will avoid using the word "never" here; however, only one to three times out of 100 they may actually want your advice. When you are sharing something, are you looking for them to tell you what you should do? I doubt it. Emotional safety and intimacy are where partners can share their thoughts and feelings. If you jump in with the "fix it tool," particularly before they finish, you will not be seen as emotionally safe. Stop doing that. Stop using the "fix it" tool. It is the wrong tool.

Instead, listen for and acknowledge their emotions: use empathy. "Wow, you seem angry about that." "You look like that really makes you sad." "That is really upsetting isn't it?" When you do this, you communicate that they are important to you, you care, you see them, you understand their experience and how it impacts them, and on and on. If you have a brilliant idea that you do not think they see, ask permission. "I have a thought on that if you are interested." "Have you thought about _____."

That is light years from, "You just need to _____."
Or, "You should _____." Those statements only cause
others to raise their defensive shields and resist you at all
costs. No one likes to be told what to do. Do you?

4.   Express Appreciation

Finally, express appreciation. Do you already say please
and thank you? If not, start right now by calling or texting
your partner and thanking them for something. They may
faint, so consider whether or not they are somewhere
appropriate first. Everyone wants to feel valued and
appreciated because we all work hard in life. Do you ever
tell your partner that? Making deposits into their self-
esteem will never hurt the relationship or your efforts to
get them to meet your needs.

What does that look like? When they do something you
do not like, I will bet you can lecture them for 20 minutes
without pausing to think. Sure, that is easy to do. Do you

lecture your children that way? Do you like it when someone lectures you? What happens when they do something right? "Thanks." "Nice job." Where is the energy going? Yes, the wrong way. Can you see how out of balance the communication is? This energy balance has to change.

What if you expressed appreciation and gratitude like this: "Hey, I wanted to thank you for making my lunch today. It was really great not having to worry about where I was going to eat. I know you have a lot to do in the morning, so thank you. When you do that for me, I feel really important to you." Now tell me, if you express appreciation for your partner that way, will life get better for you? Will your partner and your children be drawn into wanting to do more for you because it feels good to them? How would you like to be treated?

There you go: four very simple, powerful and effective things you can do right now to help your relationship start to feel better. Remember the golden rule: Do unto others, as you want others to do unto you.

LOVE AND RELATIONSHIP - ADVICE FOR COUPLES

How do you improve love and relationships? If you are in a relationship with someone you love and adore, regardless of whether you are married or not, it can bring you either sheer joy or grievous pain.

Love in any relationship brings with it many expectations and much hope. Being loved unconditionally is the paramount dream of a great many people. When you are loved unconditionally, it means you are accepted for whom and for what you are, have a sense of belonging, the feeling of being protected and safe but most of all, it means deep-rooted intimacy, romance, and passion united by an everlasting bond.

But in time, love and the relationship may get onto the wrong pathway. Hope dies and in place of love comes anger, frustration, and loneliness. When you are in the honeymoon phase of your relationship, feelings are often based on lust and the illusion that the two of you will get together as one. But as time passes by, this perfect image fades and the dream is ruined.

The fact is that the two people involved in a relationship are different. They have different needs, different expectations, and different directions. However, it is important to understand that the disenchantment that follows the discovery of this reality is expected, and is an unavoidable step on the pathway to finding true love and happiness. You just need to work on it.

Even with the best intentions, all relationships can gradually run down. Early pleasures become commonplace and boring, minor flaws become major faults, little eccentricities become really irritating. To overcome this, it is necessary to give each other little pleasures occasionally - the meaningful compliment, a phone call to say I love you, a walk hand in hand in the park, flowers or a romantic dinner are just some examples.

So, how can you improve love and relationships? Is it commitment to the strength of your romantic dream, an alignment of your value systems, appropriate communication skills or is it just a matter of luck?

Some say that the success of love and relationships is directly related to the evolutionary theory and to leadership. Leadership is the secret to a successful relationship. Males are programmed genetically to be leaders. It goes back to the caveman days and involves the hunter instinct. When a man and a woman first meet, the hunter mode is very strong in him. He shows off his leadership skills - he asks her out, pays for the meal, opens the door and asks for her hand in marriage.

Because of these biological instincts, women are subconsciously attracted to this leadership behavior - they fall head over heels in love with this potential husband, provider and potential father of their children. The truth is that this genetic programming makes sure that mankind survives.

The secret to saving a marriage lies in building attraction, not in solving problems. It is a fact that women are driven more by emotion than logic. Therefore men, if you are always apologizing, discussing, compromising, groveling or begging, it is like water off a duck's back - it just washes over a woman and may even kill the attraction you have for each other.

I am not saying that communication is not important. It goes without saying that an effective leader will have good communication skills. In all relationships or leadership roles, it is necessary to have good effective communication skills such as:

❖ Effective listening skills - Understand your partner and have empathy. Good listening makes certain that you keep in tune with your partner and see your relationship through their eyes. When you listen well to what your partner is saying, you are actually saying that you care.

❖ The ability to express your feelings properly and the ability to understand your partner's feeling without judgment. Be assertive rather than passive when expressing your emotions. Really care about what your partner is feeling.

❖ A clean communication style - Avoid things like being judgemental, blame, accusations, put-downs, threats, bringing up old history, negative comparisons. Address the action, not the person.

❖ Good negotiation skills - People negotiate with their partner constantly. It is a process where it is decided about how the things in the relationship will be done, i.e. housework, disciplining children or buying a new house. Negotiations need to be fair, allowing both partners to achieve their goals without manipulation, hurt or regret.

❖ A constructive, healthy conflict resolution method. Deal with old conflicts and resentments and put them to bed and then develop some strategies to deal with current problems effectively. Take time out if necessary to stop fights escalating into verbal or physical abuse.

It is also important to learn how to cope with anger, whether you are the aggressor or the victim because anger damages intimate relationships. Anger, which openly aggressive or disguised as passive-aggressive, creates emotional scars. These worsen with every outburst, interfering with both intimacy and trust. Emotional abuse has the same effects as physical abuse on a person.

So what do you have to do to build attraction and to develop an appropriate couple system to save your marriage? You need to work on the male's leadership skills and rekindle the hunter instinct in him so that he becomes that amazing, compelling, dynamic, charismatic leader she was attracted to at first. And then the female's biology will take care of the rest. Your sex drive will be reactivated and you will both fall wildly and madly in love again. Every argument can turn into a passionate, lovemaking session!

And the good thing is that it is never too early or too late to learn new skills which will help you to have the ideal relationship. Everyone needs to work on their relationship skills - new lovers, partnerships of several years and even partners who are already going through difficulties with the relationship and it seems that there is no hope of keeping the love and the relationship alive.

Love and relationships take hard work, but it is important to work smarter not harder on them to achieve a long, happy, passionate and successful relationship.

How To Improve Your Relationship

If you want to know how to improve your relationship, here are some simple steps that I've found will help you to create (or recreate) warmth, love, and affection between you and your significant other.

Find the Love in You!

You need to find and recognize the love in yourself before you can share it with another. Sages and Saints from all traditions have told us that Love is within us -- always and forever. The Yogis of India says there is a spot in the centre of your chest which is the gateway to an infinite ocean of Love within. Would you like to dive in? All you need to do is sit quietly with your eyes closed. Then in your mind's eye, bring up a memory of someone or something you love. Feel your loving feelings for that person and let that loving feeling bring a warm smile to your lips. Just bask in the glow of that loving feeling for a few moments. Then smile into your body, appreciating it, feeling grateful for it.

Chinese sages invented this Inner Smile technique as a form of Chi Kung to bring health and well-being to the body. We're using it to feel wonderful and to saturate our being with a sense of Love. So bring that smiling, loving energy into the centre of your chest. Imagine there is a tiny opening there in the hollow of your chest that leads to that Infinite Love within. Feel into that space and just create a sense of infinite unending Love. Enjoy it. Soak in it. And above all, know that you can access it and feel it at any time, just by placing your attention and awareness there.

Pledge Your Allegiance to Love!

Now you've discovered that eternal Love is there within you, you are free from being so needy and dependent on others for your happiness. Already you are more attractive and appealing to be around. You have plugged into Love and your energetic vibration is so much more appealing to be around.

Now, as far as how to improve your relationship goes, I think a prime secret is that 'commitment to Love' that we have all so conveniently forgotten. We've been suckered by romance movies into thinking that Love should be effortless and spontaneous. Something we experience as a happening. But Love is a verb -- it's something you DO! And you get to enjoy its incredible benefits if you work at bringing it into your life. You do that by making it a priority. And you demonstrate your commitment to that new value, by making small but highly significant changes in your behavior and the way you treat others -- particularly your spouse, children, boyfriend/girlfriend, significant other, and... what the heck, everybody else in your world! Get committed to Love and, I believe, Love gets committed to you.

The Dance with the Beloved

Make an active show of being in Love with your partner. Start saying, "I love you" frequently throughout the day whenever you are around your partner. Give unexpected hugs and kisses. Don't stand there expecting them to reciprocate. You might be doing all the 'work' to begin with -- it can be frustrating, but keep dipping into that Infinite Love within, okay?

Thank your partner whenever they do something for you and show appreciation for the things they do in life and at home. If your relationship has been at a very low ebb, this can be really arduous and hard work to begin with but you are committed to this because you want that 'loving feeling' back between you. I'm telling you to do this with your partner, but don't stop there -- spread the love through all your relationships: your children, your siblings, your parents or relatives, your friends, and co-workers. You deserve to improve all your relationships.

Symbols of Love

Now that you are all about Love, support your relationship with reminder triggers and unconscious cues. The Chinese art of Feng Shui recommends that to improve your relationship, you should put pictures of happy loving couples in your bedroom and remove any pictures of single people. You can also include those small statuettes of couples hugging and kissing. I've been in the habit of buying one on every anniversary -- and they are subconscious cues about coupledom, togetherness and intimacy.

What's in a Name?

Have you got a pet name for your loved one? When talking to your partner, if you don't already, start dropping in loving tags, like 'my darling,' 'sweetheart,' 'beloved' or 'lover.' Some people use 'baby' but do you really want to mother your partner? Same goes for calling your man 'Daddy.' Steer away from mixing your metaphors like that. Stick with equal footing terms of endearment.

Remove Your Clause

Throw away the 'escape clause' that you keep stuffed in the back of your mind. This is that thought that you can always leave this relationship if something better comes along, or can leave it if the other person doesn't conform to your idea of what the relationship should be. Resolve right now to make a go of this relationship, come hell or high water. Never again bring the threat of leaving into an argument. We've been trained by too many TV dramas into thinking that if you have an argument, it has to become this big emotional explosion that leads to dramatic separations. It's so childish. Commit to resolving differences and returning to a state of love and lessen your need to prove that you are right and the other person is wrong. Who cares! It's not worth it if it mucks up the emotional tone of your togetherness.

The Riches of Love

Invest in your relationship and it will pay the biggest and best dividends of your life. Become a love billionaire. Your search for the secrets of how to improve your relationship will be rewarded with an enriched relationship. End the hurt and disappointment, and create the love you deserve in your life. Start by copying the strategies of top 1% of couples who enjoy wonderful love-filled relationships. Discover how to never have fights again, save your marriage, and grow deeply in Love with one another.

POSSESSIVENESS - A HURDLE FOR RELATIONSHIP

Possessiveness in marriage is the desire to dominate or control every aspect of a spouse's life. It may be with regard to friendships and relationships, jobs, hobbies or even programmes that can be watched on TV. It can lead to coercive control of the other person, making the victim afraid to oppose such behavior or do what she wants to do. Possessiveness is commonly attributed to men. But there are many women who also like to keep their husbands in a vice-like grip. Probably the term 'hen-pecked' reflects this attitude.

A marriage was arranged between a smart and sprightly young pharmacist and an officer in a private bank. Though his features were distorted by Bell's palsy, the parents thought nothing of it. He had a steady job with a good income and this ensured the security of their daughter. Within a few months, the girl turned into a sad, morose and distracted woman. Her husband was possessive to the extent that she had to give him an hour by hour account of her behavior at work. He obstructed her progress professionally in different ways.

She could not join in any social activities with her colleagues. Three children followed in quick succession. The girl tolerated her husband's behavior for 10 years then she absconded, leaving a note to say that unless her husband went in for psychiatric treatment for his abnormal behavior, she would never come back again. One recalls the nursery rhyme of "Peter, Peter pumpkin eater who married a wife but couldn't keep her. So he put her in a pumpkin shell, and there he kept her very well."

But the girl broke through the shell hollering, "Don't you dare fence me in."

Obviously, his facial deformity had given him a complex. He felt that unless he controlled his wife, she would be unfaithful or even leave him. He lost her not because of his looks but because of his behavior. Timely psychiatric intervention finally brought about a reunion.

Signs of Possessive Relationships

Possessive relationships vary in severity. While some possessive individuals may try to control every aspect of their partner's life, other possessive individuals may only show mild jealousy. Regardless of the level of possessiveness, such relationships are typically unhealthy. However, spotting a possessive relationship is not always easy. It may even start out positively. Thus, partners who see warning signs may want to look closely at the relationship, even if things seem to be going well.

1.   Your Partner Disrespects You

Disrespect is often a sign of a possessive relationship. Possessive individuals may make negative comments toward you or about ex-partners. This might take the form of name-calling, rudeness, sarcasm or critical remarks. In some cases, the possessive individual's goal is to make you feel worthless and incapable of finding another relationship by damaging your self-esteem. Possessive partners may also disrespect your career or academic choices.

2.   Jealousy Abounds

A possessive person often expresses jealousy. He might become angry or upset when you socialize with friends, family or co-workers. Along with this, he may accuse you of cheating or be suspicious of innocent behaviors such as sending an email or a text message. In extreme cases, your possessive partner may try to cut off your contact with friends and family because he is jealous of the time you spend with them.

3. You Are Being Manipulated

A possessive partner uses manipulative behavior. For example, your partner might threaten to leave you if you do not do exactly what he wants. In some cases, possessive people might also self-injure, threaten suicide or engage in other self-destructive behaviors if you show interest in friends, family, hobbies, work or school. In other words, a manipulative partner may go to great lengths to ensure that you spend most of your time with him.

4. You Are Being Controlled

Controlling behaviors often signal a possessive relationship. Control can be physical, emotional or financial. A possessive partner may try to forbid you from holding a job or managing your own money. Likewise, he may try to forbid you from seeking employment, choosing your own clothing, cutting your hair or making other basic day-to-day decisions.

5.   Your Partner Has a Temper

A short temper can be a warning sign. Possessive individuals may become angry over seemingly minor incidents, such as if you arrive home 10 minutes late. In extreme cases of possessiveness, this anger might be marked by physical abuse such as shoving, punching or slapping, but also commonly involves yelling, cursing and other forms of verbal abuse.

Dealing With Possessiveness in a Relationship

The subject of having a possessive or controlling relationship partner may feel worlds away from the sweet sentiment behind asking someone to be your Valentine. However, many couples find there can be a slippery slope from desiring a lover to wanting to own them. When it comes to coping with feelings of jealousy or insecurity, couples can cross the line from love to possessiveness. They often intrude on each other's boundaries and disrespect each other's inherent independence. Think of all the secret searches through cell phones, the guilt trips when one partner goes out with friends, the outbursts when reassurance isn't offered or the interrogations over attractions to anyone else.

There are many subtle and not-so-subtle ways people attempt to control relationship partners as a means to calm their own emotions. Yet, feeling connected to someone doesn't mean it is okay to act entitled or to exert power over them. In fact, attempts to exercise power over our partners actually serve to reduce and diminish our own attraction to them. When we try to control someone close to us, we limit them in ways that make them less themselves. We want our partners (and ourselves for that matter) to be fulfilled, well-rounded individuals who are fully alive. When we make our partner feel guilty for choosing to spend time with friends, for example, we actually shrink their world. We should always aim to grow each other's worlds rather than restrict them. Otherwise, we take the air and life out of the relationship. It's no surprise that studies have shown that jealousy and surveillance behaviors we often associate with possessiveness lead to relationship dissatisfaction and destructive behavior.

So how can you stop the possessive patterns in your relationship? The first step is to understand why you engage in controlling behavior, and the second step is to deal with the underlying feelings that drive you toward an unequal dynamic.

Most of us have some degree of fear and insecurity surrounding our close relationships. These feelings can spring from deeper struggles we have with trust, low self-esteem, fears of rejection, loss or intimacy itself. These deep-seated emotions can lead to a desire to control. Instead of exploring where these feelings come from, we tend to project them onto our partner and start acting out controlling behaviors that we hope will alleviate these painful feelings.

For example, we may, on some core level, feel unlovable or like no one would ever choose us. This negative self-concept can lead us to act out all kinds of jealous or insecure behaviors with our partner. We may start giving them the cold shoulder in hopes they'll show interest in our feelings. We may act victimized and wounded by any comment or action that we can construe as disregarding or rejecting. We may outright scold our partner or make rules about where they can and can't go, what they can and can't do. All of these behavior patterns have a lot more to do with us than our partner. And most of them have deep roots in our past.

As children, we developed strategies or defenses in an effort to protect ourselves from difficult or painful conditions. These early experiences shaped our expectations about relationships and the defenses we formed then still play out in our lives today. That is why making sense of our own past and exploring our early attachment patterns can be very helpful in understanding our feelings of possessiveness as adults. For example, if

173

we experienced an anxious attachment pattern growing up, we may have felt a lot of uncertainty around getting our needs met and felt like we had to cling to our parents to make them take care of us – in essence, to survive. As adults, we may project these feelings onto our partner, feeling like we need to make things happen, remind them to notice us, etc. We may have a lot of anxiety about their movement, fearing rejection or abandonment. As a result, we relive the past, clinging or making efforts to control our partner, so we can feel secure.

Unfortunately, because these feelings are rooted in our history, we rarely, if ever, get the reassurance we seek from acting out our old defenses in the present. Instead, we repeat patterns from our childhood, acting on our insecurities, and often pushing our partner further away in the process. The patterns and defenses we form growing up may have been adaptive to our childhood, but they can hurt our current relationships. However, there are real steps we can take to break patterns of defensiveness and achieve an equal and trusting relationship.

1. **Enhance our sense of self -** If insecurity is at the root of our possessive behavior, we have to start to look at ways to bring more self-compassion into our lives. We have to take steps to overcome our inner critic and truly accept that we are worthy and okay on our own, independent of anyone. We are strong and capable. Even if our worst fears come true, and our partner does reject or betray us, we have to know that our world will not end.

2. **Resist engaging in jealous, authoritative, or punishing behaviors -** Actions like surveillance will only alienate our partner and drive a wedge between us. Plus, they lead us to feel bad about ourselves. No matter how anxious it makes us, we have to resist the urge to exert power over our partner. We have to ignore that inner

voice telling us, "Just don't talk to her. She needs to know she can't just work late and expect you to be happy." Or, "Let him know you won't stand for this. He better not think he can just goof off every weekend."

3.   **Accept that these feelings are from the past -** Our anxiety will never ease until we deal with where it's really coming from. Current events trigger old, primal pain. If we're having an especially strong desire to control or possess our partner, chances are this has something to do with our history. Making sense of our story by creating a coherent narrative of our past can lead us to a great sense of self-understanding. It can help us know our triggers and feel calmer in the present. Therapy can also be a life-changing tool when it comes to understanding and overcoming these feelings.

4.   **Find ways to calm your anxiety -** There are many methods for calming our anxiety. Mindfulness

practices and breathing exercises allow us to learn to sit with our thoughts and feelings without being overpowered by them or allowing them to control our behavior.

5.   **Oust your inner critic -** We all have a "critical inner voice" that attacks us and those close to us, often sabotaging our relationships. This critic feeds us thoughts like, "She's probably cheating on you." "Who would love you anyway?" "He's just going to leave you." This critic is often at the wheel when we experience relationship anxiety, distorting our thinking and encouraging us to engage in possessive behavior. You can read more about how to identify and stand up to your inner critic here.

6.   **Invest in your life -** One of the most important steps we can take when dealing with possessive feelings and impulses is to focus on our own life. Ask "What lights me up? What do I like to do?" We should try to shift our attention off our partner and start thinking

about all the things that we're interested in pursuing – that would enhance our sense of who we are as independent individuals.

7.   **Talk to your partner from an adult perspective** - It can be valuable to have an open and honest conversation with our partner in which we disclose our struggle with insecurity and feelings that we need to control the situation. We can commit to trying not to act on these feelings, but let our partner know what's going on within us, so we can feel closer to them. While any attempts to control or induce guilt may make our partner feel resentful or annoyed, an open conversation in which we don't lay blame, but explain our personal struggle is a vulnerable act that will often allow our partner to understand us and feel for us.

When it comes to relationships, we are always better off trusting our partner and being hurt than restricting them.

This is the only way we can truly know that we are loved and chosen by a free person. By enhancing our sense of self, enjoying our independence and truly appreciating the real closeness we feel with someone we love, we can be self-possessed within ourselves. That way, no matter what the outcome, we benefit because we've acted with integrity and stayed true to ourselves, qualities that will serve us well in the long haul of any relationship.

Possessiveness in a Relationship Will Poison It - Let Your Partner Make Their Own Choices

Your partner has decided to end your relationship because you are too possessive. You may feel shocked by the announcement but if you retrace your steps, you will see a pattern unfold.

When your boyfriend is with other girls, how do you react? Do you join the party and get to know them or do you sulk and tell the girls to get away from your man?

179

This will not only infuriate your partner but the girls as well.

As men and women, we often have friends from both sexes, as it is all part of our human growth. If you cannot bear your partner talking, let alone laughing with another woman then it is no wonder you are alone. When you are possessive, you are literally suffocating the person you say you love. You are giving them no trust that they can choose their own friends. So what if one of the girls is coming onto your boyfriend? There is no need for you to start a fight. If your boyfriend really loves you, he might be flattered by her approaches but it is you he wants to be with. You are going to make a lot of enemies if you verbally attack every girl who flirts with your guy.

It is as though you want to own him. Maybe you want to lock him up in his house when you are not around. You are bordering on being obsessive and the next step after that is stalking. You are going to have to work on this problem because it can be dangerous. What if one of these girls physically attacked you? Trying to run this guy's life has made you lose him. He obviously valued his freedom more than you.

You may need help with this, as the problem can be deep-rooted. You may have seen your father being a controlling man with your mother as he somehow did not feel deserving of her. That fear that everyone in your life will disappear keeps happening because of your unresolved issues.

Counseling can be an excellent way to put things in perspective but if you do not feel comfortable with that then changing your view of relationships is essential. A partner is not a possession. They are a person with thoughts and feelings of their own and a right to their own choices. It is not your job to change them. We meet and fall in love with other people's uniqueness and often the differences we share are what makes us attractive to them. However, you want to steal that from a partner and control them constantly.

Take a hard look at your relationships and see why and how they ended. It was your possessiveness that drove them away and made them think you were a bit crazy. What is so hard about enjoying who a person is and not trying to alter them in any way?

We have addressed the problem and you know you cannot go on this way. You cannot even think about contacting your ex until you have worked on this. Love is about being free to be and accepting your love for who they are. Bite the bullet and when you see your ex talking to some girls, walk up and say hi and leave. If your ex can see you are making an effort, he may still be interested. You have to stop seeing every person as a threat to your relationship.

Building your self-esteem is another thing you need to work on. Stop believing it would be so easy for another girl to take a guy away from you. Believe in yourself. He chose you after all. Every time you feel this stuff rising up in your throat, breathe deeply as it is a simple an effective way to calm yourself down. You have learned this negative behavior, now you need to unlearn it. It can be done and you will feel as if a big weight has been lifted off your shoulders. When you love someone, it should be the happiest time of your life, not the most anxious and burdened. Do not try to get back with your ex till you have worked on your problems. Give him and yourself time. When you are ready, he will get a girl who has worked hard and is a lot lighter and free. If you think this guy could be your soulmate then your lesson is to let go of the pain in your heart. Only then will you be free to love.

ANXIETY SERIES

Anxiety in Relationship has been the first book in the "Anxiety Series", best seller in its category, still today…

The second publication was The Attachment Theory Workbook - How to Eliminate Insecurity in Love, Jealousy, Conflicts and Better Understand your Partenr's Mind. Build a Strong Relationship!

My last effort is Anxious in Love - How Stopping the Spiral of Toxic Thoughts and Anxiety in Relationship Overcoming Conflicts and Insecure of Couple. Abandonment and Separation is Never a Relief! …after many months of absence from publications.

For better enjoyment, you can find all the titles in audio format, on Audible, please!

MY FREE STEP-BY-STEP HELP

<u>I'll send you a free eBook</u>! Yes, you got it right, I'll send you my future projects, in preview, with nothing in return, if you just want a realistic review on them, which I'm sure will be useful to me. Thanks in advance!

Leave me your best email, my staff will send you a copy as soon as possible:

theresamillerauthor@gmail.com

Do not go yet; One last thing to do…

If you enjoyed this book or found it useful I'd be very grateful if you'd post a short review on Amazon. Your support really does make a difference and I read all the reviews personally so I can get your feedback and make this book even better.

Thanks again for your support !